Per Petersson

Ola Johansson

Martin Broman

Dan Blücher

Henric Alsterman

With examples from
Manufacturing, Administration,
Services and Healthcare

Lean

– Turn *Deviations* into Success!

Lean – Turn Deviations into Success!

ISBN 978-91-633-4587-6
1st issue

Cover: Åsa Plahn, Poise Graphics/Wickholm Form
Layout: Svante Ahlsén, Illustrator AB
Sketches: Svante Ahlsén, Illustrator AB
Other illustrations: Part Development AB
Publishing house: Part Media, Grönviksvägen 185, SE-167 76 Bromma, Sweden
Printed by: Kristianstads Boktryckeri AB, Kristianstad, Sweden 2010

www.partdevelopment.com

Contents

Foreword

Numerous books on Lean have been written since the book "The Machine that Changed the World" was published in 1990. This, of course, raises the question: why do we see the need for yet another one? The answer is that the Lean discussion in many organizations is still too technical in nature and mainly focused on various support functions' use of Lean methods, or Lean tools, as some prefer to denote them. There is definitely nothing wrong with these Lean methods; many organizations have achieved great results with them. The problem is that far too many practitioners lack the fundamental understanding of what Lean *actually* means. Unsystematic application of Lean methods is a common result and the methods are often introduced as drives. When there is a weak connection between the actual problem and the choice of methods, there is a risk that lasting results will fail to materialize.

As an attempt to avoid this problem, this book brings an understanding of the importance of detecting deviations and, through concrete improvements based on the Lean principles, making sure that they will not recur. This book is for established Lean practitioners as well as for those who have not yet started their journey towards Lean. It is moreover suitable as a students' guide.

This book is written primarily from a manufacturing perspective but it also contains explanatory examples from administration, services and healthcare operations. The examples show that Lean is equally applicable to all types of processes and flows. There are many similarities between a manufacturing flow and e.g. an administrative flow. In both cases there are products that are refined through a number of process steps so as to meet an agreed specification. The difference between manufacturing flows and administrative flows is that it may be harder to identify administrative products and value streams. However, it is obvious that they exist and that they can be improved!

The content of this book is based on research as well as on experience from many years of practical application of Lean in a number of different operations and industries. In this book we provide *our* view of what Lean is, what effects it can bring, and what it requires from an organization.

Stockholm in February 2010

Per Petersson

Ola Johansson

Martin Broman

Dan Blücher

Henric Alsterman

Reader's Guide

Chapter 1: Why Lean?

This opening chapter provides a comprehensive description of changing business demands and how Lean – as a way of relating to operations – can contribute to meeting these demands. The chapter is recommended for those readers who want to understand how Lean affects competitiveness.

Chapter 2: The History of Lean

This chapter describes periods of the last 100 years of industrial history that have proven to be important for what is nowadays called Lean. The chapter provides interesting trivia for those readers who want to understand where the thoughts within Lean surfaced and why.

Chapter 3: Guiding Principles

Lean is built on two main principles. These are described along with basic principles and important basic conditions. The chapter is important for understanding what a Lean effort ideally strives to achieve and it is therefore recommended for all readers.

Chapter 4: Standardization – Reveals Waste

This chapter describes what standardization means and why it is important. It focuses on the standardization of manual work and is recommended to all readers as it provides an understanding of the importance of defining the details of the operations.

Chapter 5: Improvement Work – The Key to Success

This chapter covers various kinds of improvement work. The crucial importance of the improvement work for an organization to succeed with Lean is also discussed. The chapter is recommended for all readers.

Chapter 6: The Value Stream – The Improvement Arena

Here Lean is discussed from a flow perspective. Improving individual processes is important, but to achieve maximum profit from the Lean effort all processes have to be linked together into a smooth flow. The chapter is recommended for all readers.

Chapter 7: Towards the Goal

This chapter deals with the problems that can arise when a business is striving for Lean but is measured and evaluated the traditional way. Lean is about long-term success and thus requires that evaluations and calculations are adapted accordingly. Otherwise, there is a great risk that wrong decisions will be made. The chapter is recommended for all readers.

Chapter 8: Crossroad Thoughts

Some frequently asked questions are answered in order to provide support for the decision on whether to go for Lean or not. The chapter is primarily intended for those readers who feel uncertain about whether or not Lean is the right path for them to follow.

Appendix: A Small Selection of Lean Methods

The appendix contains a discussion on the importance of understanding what has to be done, and why, before a method is chosen to solve a problem or a task. In addition, the appendix contains descriptions of five common Lean methods and it is intended for those readers who want to get an insight into what a Lean method can be like.

Glossary

The glossary at the end of the book serves as a work of reference to describe the various terms and acronyms used in this book.

Lean cannot be "implemented". Instead, Lean is a stepwise approach towards a vision where all waste is eliminated.

1. Why I

Why Lean?

The term Lean Production is widely spread but the opinions on what it *actually* means vary. To some people Lean Production means using a method that is classified as "Lean", while others view it as a strategy comprising every activity within a company. Henceforth in this book Lean Production will be referred to as Lean.

Lean has a long history of application to manufacturing activities. In recent years, however, the number of applications of Lean thinking outside the manufacturing field has increased rapidly. Healthcare provides a good example showing that Lean is applicable to any kind of operation. All activities at a hospital should aim at creating value for the patients being treated.

Lean is not an activity or method where simple implementation means that the work is done. Rather, it is a state-of-mind or a way to relate to how operations are performed, or a strategy for how to run the operation. Thus, Lean is a higher-ranking term that comprises company culture, values, basic principles, methods, leadership, co-workership, etc. Lean cannot be "implemented". Instead, Lean is a stepwise approach towards a vision where *all* waste is eliminated. This, of course, is not possible in practice.

Lean is a way of relating to operations that provides great opportunities for increased profitability and competitiveness through increased productivity and flexibility. However, in certain ways prevailing conditions in the business world seem both to help and to hinder a successful Lean effort.

Increasing Demands

A company experiences demands from a number of parties. It should be attractive to investors (and other financiers) while being an excellent supplier to its customers. In a global and deregulated market it is even more important to meet customers' demands, as competition increases when more potential suppliers compete for the same customers.

Investor demand for frequent reports has also increased. Previously an annual report showing financial progress was enough for large and medium sized companies. There was also a period when bi-annual reports were demanded while now quarterly reports are the norm. A problem with frequent reporting is that it implies that company efforts should pay off rapidly and that their effects are presumed to impact the next quarterly report. There is a considerable risk that this kind of short-term thinking counteracts long-term success. Critics say that quarterly reports make company management focus more on short-term changes in share value than on the company's long-term development.

Demands from customers also increase in most branches of business. These demands are sometimes expressed using one-way communication: the customer tells the supplier what to do and the supplier has no other choice than to agree. In these cases there is a lack of insight about the fact that the strongest supply chain is the most profitable. Customers alone dictate conditions instead of cooperating with the suppliers to find solutions that will bring mutual profitability. A common consequence is low profitability for the supplier and unreliable deliveries for the customer, which in turn results in problems and increased total costs for both.

Productivity as a Competitive Tool

Increased productivity is a common denominator in satisfying investor demands as well as customer demands. There appears to be a great potential for improvement in this area. Some researchers and company managers in Western manufacturing industries claim that there is a potential to increase productivity by 50 per cent in many Western companies (2008). In addition, there are indications that the productivity potential in operations outside manufacturing may be even bigger.

The most manifest threat when productivity is too low is that operations are transferred to low-cost countries. Today, this threat is also a reality in operations outside manufacturing. The arguments for moving operations to low-cost countries are normally based on the belief that lower wages will lead to increased profitability and/or increased competitiveness. There are even examples of customers demanding that their suppliers move their operations to low-cost countries as this is expected to result in reduced prices. Unfortunately, this kind of discussion disregards the fact that the potential gains in profits due to lower wage levels are often eliminated by costs related to longer lead times, increased tied-up capital, poor control, increased shipping costs, etc. These are drawbacks that can be difficult to quantify in advance, but fair estimations need to reflect a holistic view.

James P. Womack, one of the authors of "The Machine that Changed the World", contributed to the spreading interest for Lean around the world. In one of his newsletters (2003), he listed the following factors that should be considered before operations are moved to low-cost countries.

Factors to Consider before a Relocation Decision, according to J.P. Womack

- The piece part cost for an item where you are
- The piece part cost for the same item in the proposed location (e.g. China or India)
- The cost of slow freight to get it to your customer
- The overhead costs allocated to production in the high-wage location, which usually do not disappear when production is transferred. Instead they are re-allocated to remaining products, raising their apparent cost.

- The cost of additional inventory of goods in transit over long distances from the low-wage location to the customer
- The cost of expensive expedited shipments
- The cost of warranty claims if the new facility or supplier has a long learning curve
- The cost of engineer visits or resident engineers to get the process right so the product is made to the correct specification with acceptable quality
- The cost of senior executive visits to set up the operation or to straighten out relationships with managers and suppliers operating in a different business environment
- The cost of out-of-stocks and lost sales caused by long lead times to obtain the part
- The cost of remaindered goods or of scrapped stocks, ordered to a long-range forecast and never actually needed
- The potential cost, if you are using a contract manufacturer in the low-cost location, of your supplier soon becoming your competitor
- Currency risks which can strike quite suddenly when the currency of either the supplying or receiving country shifts
- Country risks which can also emerge suddenly when there is a political reaction in the receiving country as trade deficits and unemployment emerge as political issues
- Connectivity costs of many sorts in managing hand-offs and information flows in highly complex supply chains across long distances in countries with different business practices

In this list, however, the important question about the potential for improvement in existing operations is missing. From a holistic perspective the most productive operation is normally also the most competitive and profitable one in the long term. This means that if only some of the potential increases in productivity are achieved, many decisions to move operations to low-cost countries should never be made.

From Demands to Possibilities

Lean is an approach to operations that specifically aims at increasing productivity in order to attract customers as well as investors. However, it is not a miracle cure that will work wonders in the short term. Instead, it is a long-term approach that basically concerns efficient resource utilization by eliminating waste, increasing workforce commitment and focusing on relevant issues by considering the whole but working on the details.

The ideas within Lean, together with a focus on details, provide increased awareness of an organization's possibilities and limitations. This helps the organization to realize its role in the supply chain and use this increased awareness in customer relations. It provides excellent conditions for a more objective, factual debate aimed at creating an efficient flow that is beneficial to both parties.

These arguments tend to influence also the discussions about moving operations to low-cost countries. Decisions that were all too often based solely on differences in wage levels are more balanced today as companies tend to look more to the consequences for *the whole* flow, and increasingly take into account the potentials for improvement in existing operations.

The stock market may be the most difficult stakeholder to satisfy, but the results that are likely to come from a structured Lean effort ought to be attractive, at least to investors who have a fairly long investment horizon.

Positive Effects of a Lean Effort

A successful Lean effort requires that there is a real connection between Lean and the parameters of the company's competitiveness. Examples of such parameters that are positively affected by a successful Lean effort are:

- Quality
- Cost
- Flexibility
- Delivery reliability
- Delivery time

In addition to these kinds of concrete results there are other positive effects of Lean that have more to do with strengthening the workforce's well-being, driving force, motivation and influence. Examples of such effects are:

- Reduced stress
- Increased competence
- Improved cooperation
- Reduced frustration
- Improved customer communication
- Holistic understanding
- Broader and more developing tasks
- Improved safety at the workplace
- Job security

These positive effects are important in order for Lean to be successful in the long run; there has to be something in it for everyone.

Success Factors

The single most important success factor is the organization's attitude to, and understanding of, Lean. There is no quick fix to rapidly get radical improvements in results. Instead, one must accept a way of relating to operations where the road to success leads through hard work.

It should be mentioned that there are methods within Lean that can bring rapid results in limited areas. However, in the long term Lean concerns changing mindsets and providing better conditions for managers and members of the workforce to discover and reduce waste in operations. Waste can be found not only in individual processes but also in flows. Physical changes in flows (such as a new layout) are often valuable but they will not bring lasting improvements unless Lean understanding and ways of working are well established in the organization.

The terms flow and value stream are used synonymously in this book. Value stream refers to the whole that comprises and connects all processes and activities that define the product (physical, administrative, etc.) as it progresses from the first process to the last. Within e.g. healthcare the terms process and flow are sometimes used synonymously. However, in this book the term process is defined as a part of, or an activity in, a flow. The design of the value stream has a significant effect on internal efficiency as well as on customer satisfaction.

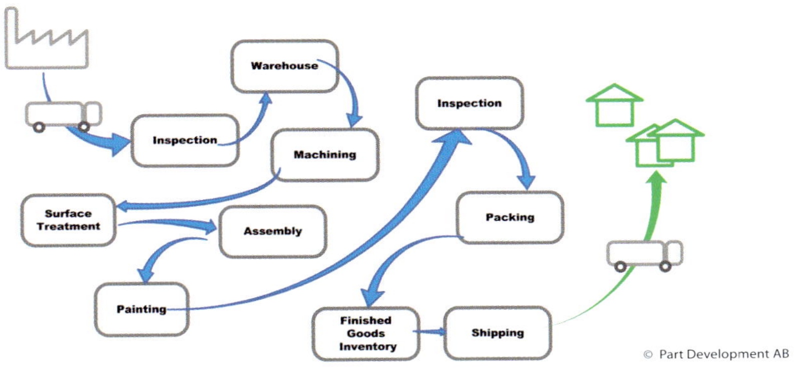

Figure 1-1. *Example of a value stream within manufacturing.*

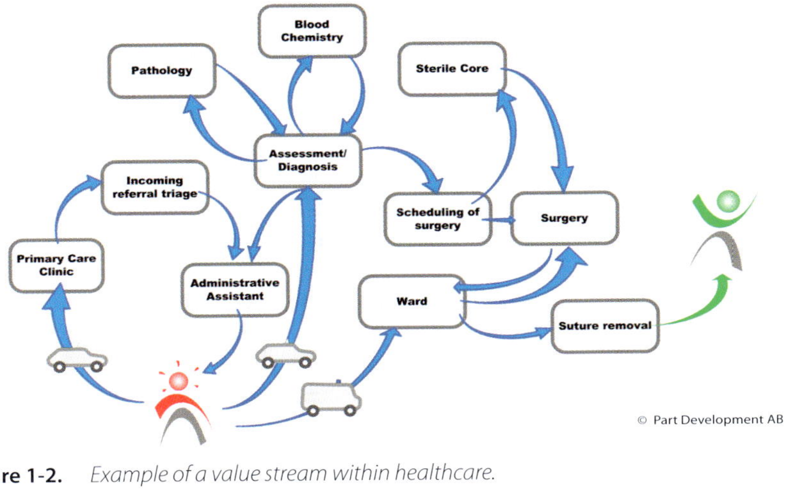

Figure 1-2. *Example of a value stream within healthcare.*

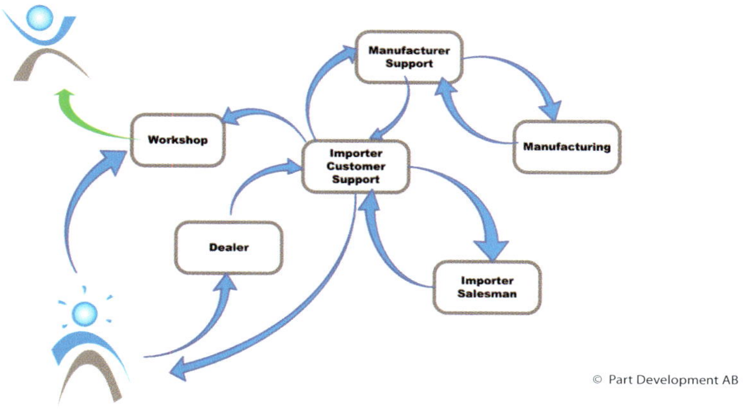

Figure 1-3. *Example of a value stream within services.*

Being successful with Lean implies achieving a state where elements such as leadership, co-workership, flows, processes, methods, etc. work together as a whole. Improvements are made while considering what is beneficial for the operation as a whole and improvements are made every day, not as occasional campaigns. Everyone participates in the improvement work carried out at Genba (Japanese term for the place where value is added).

Stakeholders

Lean aims to create the best possible whole from a large number of discrete elements affecting the whole. This holistic view also comprises the organization's stakeholders, i.e. those who in some way are affected by how operations are run. Four groups of stakeholders are usually recognized (see Figure 1-4).

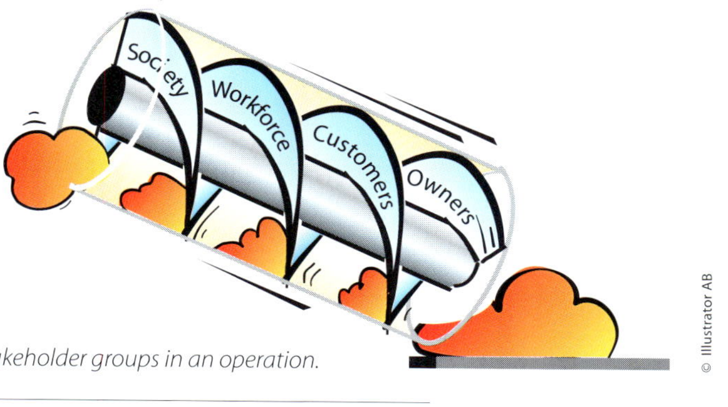

Figure 1-4. *Stakeholder groups in an operation.*

Customers are those who buy or use what is produced. This can be physical products (e.g. a TV), administrative products (e.g. a balance sheet), services (e.g. a stay at a hotel) or healthcare (e.g. treatment of a patient). It should be noted that healthcare and administration are both special cases of service operations.

In industry the customer is a stakeholder who, historically, has significantly influenced most businesses. In healthcare, however, the concept customer is often ambiguous. Sometimes the customer is considered to be the entity which purchases the service. However, this view is now changing towards seeing the patient as the actual customer.

The workforce's competence and commitment set the conditions for an organization's ability to perform. The importance of the workforce as a stakeholder has not always been given the consideration it deserves. In organizations that have progressed far on their journey towards Lean the workforce is considered to be the key to the development of the operation.

The owners are of course also important stakeholders in all types of businesses. If they are not convinced that operations are developing in the right direction, it will be difficult to raise the capital needed to run and improve the business.

Society in general is a stakeholder that has increased in importance in recent years. One reason is the environmental debate that has recently gained in strength. It is important that the development of the operation is in line with the values prevailing within society. These include humanitarian issues, politico-economical issues, environmental issues, etc. Through the educational system society is also an important supplier of competent manpower to companies and other organizations.

It is fundamental within Lean that the interests of all these four stakeholder groups are considered simultaneously. This means that when developing a new solution to a problem, a good balance between the respective concerns of these groups should be achieved so as to make the solution successful in the long term.

Some of the Lean principles have been gradually developed since the industrial revolution in the beginning of the 20th century.

2. The

The History of Lean

Lean has become increasingly popular in recent years, but the thoughts within Lean are not new. Some of the Lean principles have been gradually developed since the industrial revolution in the beginning of the 20th century. Thinkers like Benjamin Franklin, Frank Gilbreth and Frederick Winslow Taylor inspired Henry Ford in the creation of an efficient vehicle manufacturing system.

The Development of the Assembly Line

Henry Ford built his first engine in 1896 and it was used to propel a frame with four bicycle wheels. This was the first Ford.

Figure 2-1. *The first Ford (Bettmann/Corbis/Scanpix).*

In 1899 Ford founded the short-lived Detroit Automobile Company which went bankrupt after one year. The Ford Motor Company was founded three years later and it started operations by producing a few vehicles a day. The company produced the cars in the same way as its competitors did in those days, i.e. one car at a time, with all parts being brought to the car which remained stationary during assembly. Later on, Ford changed this work procedure so that the cars were moved between the various assembly teams. At the time the assembly process required a great deal of craftsmanship in fitting the parts together. The rate of assembly was relatively low and the cars were so expensive that only a few well-to-do people could afford them.

Henry Ford's goal was to produce a car that most people could afford. To achieve this, low-cost production was necessary and he realized that this required high-volume production. Ford came to see that standardization would facilitate the training of personnel as well as making the vehicles easier to assemble. The introduction of the Model T in 1908 marked the beginning of volume production.

An important element was to focus on quality: by ensuring that as many components as possible were correctly made, the subsequent manufacture and assembly became very much easier. Other distinguishing features in the Model T manufacturing process were thrift, exchangeable parts, division of labor, focus on short lead times in the entire value stream, and careful quality control in the manufacturing flow. Due to Ford's focus on quality it was possible to install the engine in the vehicle without a preceding engine test. Thus, the engine was tested for the first time when the vehicle was about to leave the factory, while his competitors had to test all engines before they were installed into vehicles. The notion of appropriate level of quality at all stages, which Ford had conceptualized already in the beginning of the 20th century, is today a Lean principle. Apart from the fact that Ford's way of producing cars was very efficient, the division of labor also enabled rapid and easy interchange of individuals in the workforce as well as making their training easier. This way of thinking eventually led to the first assembly line, introduced at Ford's Highland Park factory outside Detroit, in 1913.

Figure 2-2. *Model T assembly line at the Highland Park factory (Corbis/Scanpix).*

An interesting novelty at Highland Park, in addition to the assembly line, was the method that fed the assembly line with parts. The parts were delivered in a flow, one piece at a time, to their correct positions along the assembly line. Henry Ford's vision was that every part and every product in the factory would be in constant motion. Much later, this conception came to be one of the principles of the Toyota Production System (TPS).

The work set-up in Highland Park enabled the manufacture of high-quality cars at a low cost and with short lead times. One reason for this was that Takt was applied to the manufacturing flow. The assembly time for a car was reduced from 728 minutes to 93 minutes. Early on, Ford recognized the importance of reducing change-over times in machining as the change-overs in themselves do not add value.

That "customers could have their Model T in any color they wanted as long as it was black" is a well known quotation today. One of the reasons behind the quotation was that black paint had the shortest drying time. This was beneficial for the value stream. As only one type and one color was available Henry Ford could "relatively easily" create an efficient value stream. At the time it was the vendors' market, so there was always a customer for every Model T that came off the assembly line.

Changing Market Demands

General Motors, a Ford competitor already in the early 20th century, offered their customers a wider variety of products than Ford was able to offer with his standardized set-up. This eventually led to changing customer demands, which in turn forced Ford to abandon his successful flow orientation of the entire supply chain. A new factory, The Rouge, was built in 1928. Henry Ford's new vision was to own the entire value stream: mining, glassworks, necessary transports and everything else that is needed when producing a vehicle. Ford even owned the rubber plantation in Brazil that supplied rubber for tire manufacture. In 1930 over 100.000 people worked in this value stream. The magnitude of the undertaking can be illustrated by the fact that Ford had his own railway with 16 engines to take care of all transport of materials.

High-volume manufacturing and the possibility of being able to provide customers with a wide freedom of choice was in focus at The Rouge. The assembly line was similar to that at Highland Park, but the machining was functionally oriented and focus was shifted to high utilization of the machines and to economies of scale through high volumes. Machining was centrally controlled and to compensate for variations in customer demand and unpredictable material supplies, large buffers were required at retailers as well as in the manufacturing process. What Ford had called flow production in 1914 had now become mass production.

Figure 2-3. *Functionally arranged machining at The Rouge (Bettmann/Corbis/Scanpix).*

From the beginning of his industrial career Henry Ford thought in ways that we would today call Lean, at least when it comes to the material flow (but definitely not when it comes to the conditions of the workforce). As he increased volumes and increased the number of models and versions, he abandoned the successful concept he had once developed. The new set-up was successful at the start, but problems surfaced already before Ford's death. The manufacturing process was too complicated and too expensive.

Jidoka is Developed in Japan

At the end of the 19th century, Sakichi Toyoda established Japan's first weaving company and in 1918 he started the Toyoda Spinning and Weaving Company. In addition to the weaving business, Toyoda also developed looms. One of his goals was to develop an automatic loom and as a first step he introduced Japan's first "motorized" loom in 1896. One of the main problems with automatic looms was the breaking of threads. If a thread breaks and the loom does not stop, the defect is woven into the fabric. It is a well-known fact that looms cannot be reversed.

In 1924 Sakichi Toyoda introduced an automatic loom. What made it unique was a built-in, patented system that halted the loom automatically when a thread broke. In this way defective fabrics could be avoided. The idea was simple and brilliant. A metal loop was attached to each thread and when a thread broke, the metal loop fell down on a switch that made the machine stop. The thread could then be repaired and the machine restarted. This machine not only automated manual work but it could also, by itself, indicate when something went wrong and then stop immediately (which made it possible to decouple man from machine). This was unique and one of the main principles of TPS, Jidoka (Autonomation), got its name from this concept. To stop production immediately when a fault occurs is the idea of one of the principles in Jidoka. In 1926 a new company was formed, Toyoda Automatic Loom Works, and the following year an assembly line was introduced at Toyoda's loom factory.

The automatic loom patent was sold in 1929 to the British company Platt Brothers & Co Ltd for £100.000. Using this money as start-up capital, Sakichi's son Kiichiro created an automotive division within Toyoda. Within this division a petrol engine prototype was developed and in 1935 the first prototype vehicle was built. When the Toyota Motor Company was established two years later, the name Toyota was chosen to distinguish the company from the Toyoda family.

The Birth of the Toyota Production System

Before the Toyoda automotive business started, Kiichiro visited a number of automotive plants in the United States as well as in Europe, Ford being one of them. After these study tours Kiichiro understood that there was a lot to learn from mass production but he also realized that what he had seen had to be adapted to Japanese conditions.

Kiichiro Toyoda's ambitions in trying to achieve maximum productivity were as high as Henry Ford's, but the conditions in Japan were completely different. Japan was poor and there was no market for a single mass produced model. The challenge was therefore to be able to produce not only small volumes of cars of various models but also to build trucks. For financial reasons, Toyoda had to create a manufacturing set-up with short lead times in which the time span from the arrival of the material at the factory until the car was sold was as short as possible. This way of reasoning also existed at the time the Model T was produced. Another requirement was that the manufacturing system should be able to produce different models and variants with limited investments in machines and tools. It was therefore important to manufacture a part only when it was needed and then to deliver it at the right time, i.e. Just-In-Time (JIT). JIT is one of the main principles within TPS.

Toyota's plant manager Taiichi Ohno studied Henry Ford's work in depth in order to be able to adapt his ideas to Japanese conditions. Ford had created a manufacturing set-up based on the exchangeability of parts as well as of people. After a few profitable years at the assembly line the workers could leave the factory. At that point they were often worn out but they had earned enough money to e.g. buy a tractor and start a farming business. This was not an option for Toyota. Ever since Japan had lost the Second World War the country's financial situation had been very weak. Toyota suffered a financial crisis resulting in decreased wages at the same time as the company was demanding increased speed of manufacturing as well as increased flexibility.

At the end of the 1940s the work of Taiichi Ohno resulted, among other things, in the structured framework of principles that is called the Toyota Production System (TPS). The first product-oriented flows were created in 1947 and JIT was disseminated to Toyota's suppliers in 1963.

Lean Production is Introduced

The oil crisis at the beginning of the 1970s hit the world's industries hard. Toyota made the necessary changes successfully and after the crisis they were considerably more profitable than their Japanese competitors. As a result, the knowledge of the benefits of TPS started to spread in Japan.

In 1979 a research program to study the differences between automotive manufacturers around the world was initiated at the Massachusetts Institute of Technology (MIT) in the United States. After many years and a number of research reports, significant differences had been found between Toyota and Western automotive manufacturers in terms of quality and productivity. The result of the study was presented in the book "The Machine that Changed the World" (Womack, Jones and Roos, 1990), and this is also the book where the term Lean Production was introduced.

The term Lean comes from Toyota's way of production, which is considered "slim and flexible". Lean is sometimes referred to as meagre or skinny, but this is not correct. Resource efficient is a better term as it concerns utilizing the available resources in the best possible way.

Lean, as it is understood today, has shown to be totally superior to mass production. To be competitive as well as profitable, every organization has to ensure that they use their resources efficiently and continuously strive to reduce waste.

This realization is now also being spread within the healthcare sector, which in the 1960's started its reorganization towards a functional set-up driven by a belief in the excellence of mass production. Various functions such as radiotherapy and surgery were centralized with the aim to improve efficiency in each process. The result was patients having to move to and fro between the resources. With Lean as the guiding star, an increasing number of organizations within healthcare are beginning to analyze their operations based on what is most beneficial for the flow and not for the specific processes, i.e. they are moving towards flow orientation.

Everyone probably agrees that waste should be eliminated, but the question is how.

3. Guidi

Guiding Principles

Lean concerns the untiring strive to eliminate waste. It is accomplished through a continuous effort to visualize and resolve the deviations in an operation. A deviation is something that deviates from what is normal and can be viewed as defined and specific waste. Everyone probably agrees that waste should be eliminated, but the question is *how*. Here Lean principles have an important task in providing guidance. For an organization's Lean effort to be successful it is necessary that the values of the organization are aligned with the Lean principles.

Values

Values reflect the organization's intended way of relating to their stakeholders. Values require certain behavior in the organization and the attained results should satisfy the stakeholders. Within Lean there is a desire to steer the organization through common values instead of formulating exactly what to do. In this way the employees are given the possibility to make their own decisions guided by the common values. Thus, the values are important in guiding the organization in the desired direction. An organization without firmly based and communicated values runs the risk of being unfocused, difficult to control and ineffective.

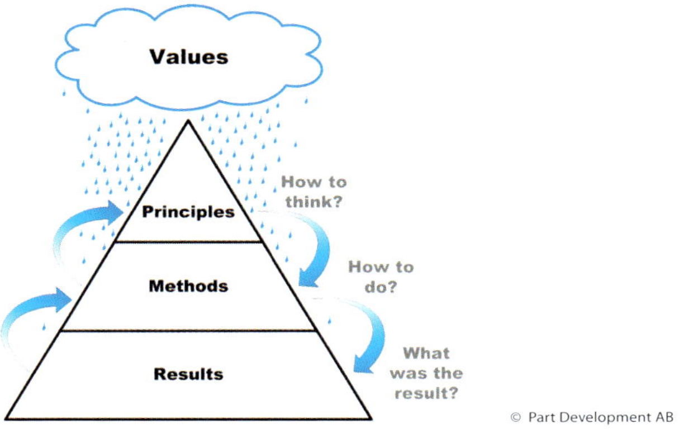

Figure 3-1. *Values permeate the entire operation and influence how the organization thinks and acts, enabling results that satisfy the stakeholders.*

What determines whether an activity develops towards Lean or "mean" is largely dependent on the organization's values and how well they are fulfilled. Respect for the workforce must be maintained, which means that it should not be unduly challenged. However, it is also undesirable to develop solutions that exclusively benefit the employees. There has to be a certain amount of pressure on the organization in order to fully satisfy customers and funders. Thus, for a solution to be sustainable a good balance between the various stakeholder interests is required.

Values do not emerge over a day, but evolve slowly over time based on the corporate culture. Culture is the foundation and soul of the organization, and has its origin in the organization's history and experiences. Therefore values normally remain unchanged over long periods. However, if relationships to the stakeholders change, or need to be changed in order for the organization to survive in its environment, then the values need to be revised.

An organization's principles must be consistent with its values but the latter must always take precedence. Values play an important role as guidelines when choosing between alternative solutions. The solution that is best for the organization is the one that creates the best balance between the values. Values can be viewed as a description of why the organization exists, while the principles describe the strategy that should be followed. Values are fixed but the principles can change. It should, however, be stressed that principles are also long-term in nature. An example is that Toyota still operates after the principles that were formulated in the middle of the 20th century. These principles are termed the Lean principles.

Values thus provide the framework of the business while the Lean principles are somewhat more specific and indicate ways of thinking to find solutions within this framework. In order to bring these ways of thinking into practice, methods are required. The human dream of flying can serve as an example of the relationship between values, principles and methods. Many people dream of being free to travel unhindered over land and sea. This dream could be compared to a human value and flying would then be a principle supporting that value. To achieve this principle a method is required. There are a number of alternative methods to attain this principle that are more or less appropriate depending on how far you want to fly and what risks you are willing to take.

Figure 3-2. *There are a number of alternative methods of flying.*

Principles – Ways of Thinking

Fundamental to Lean is that principles steer organizational management. These principles provide guidelines for how the company wants to pursue its operations. A principle is a way of thinking. Thus, it does not tell how a problem should be solved, but instead it indicates the criteria for what a proper solution should be like. Another way of putting this is that the principles guide the employees towards solutions that are correct from a Lean perspective.

In Chapter 2 it was made clear that the thoughts within Lean have been refined by Toyota in Japan. Activities inside Toyota are based on a few vital principles that were originally applied to manufacturing activities but now permeate the entire company all the way to the dealers.

A common way of communicating the Lean principles within a company is to create a visual Lean model. These Lean models usually have the shape of houses. This is because Toyota, decades ago, visualized the successful Toyota Production System (TPS) as a temple. The temple shape symbolizes stability, with the roof representing the vision of what should be achieved, while the pillars represent the TPS principles that guide the operations towards fulfilling this vision.

In Lean literature, as well as in the business world, a number of different interpretations of the TPS temple have been developed over the years. In this book we want to let the discussions start from a Lean model that is as close as possible to the original TPS temple. This Lean model only contains the vision, the main principles, and the principles within TPS.

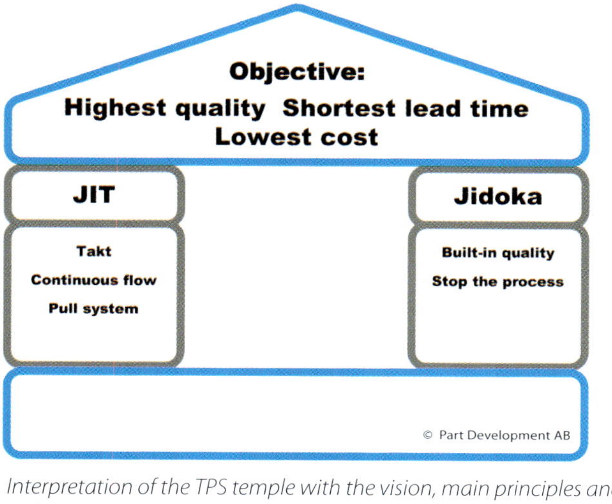

Figure 3-3. *Interpretation of the TPS temple with the vision, main principles and principles within TPS.*

The point of visualizing the principles as this kind of structure is that it makes the principles easier to memorize and easier to propagate within the organization. This has been misunderstood in far too many organizations. In those cases the creation of a Lean model is considered as proof that the organization "is Lean". The truth is instead that it is a very early step in facilitating the actual work of striving for Lean.

The different kinds of Lean models discussed here are often presented from the bottom up, the logic being that the construction of a house starts with its foundation. After that, the walls and the roof can be assembled. There is nothing wrong with this kind of simile but an important detail is missed in the discussion. Before construction starts, a building permit is required. When it comes to Lean, this building permit is the management's conviction and consent. If management has not decided to go for Lean it is not advisable to start at all. Normally, working with Lean does not lead to rapid results that bring immediate positive effects on the financial result. And, if management is not convinced and in agreement there is a risk that the effort will be shut down before the power of Lean becomes visible.

The two pillars of the Lean model represent the main principles of TPS:

- Just-In-Time (JIT)
- Jidoka

The roof of the Lean model constitutes a vision in the form of a vague world-class goal. This is a symbol for striving for perfection through continuous improvements. Sometimes this is viewed as a main principle as the continuous striving to improve operations is a fundamental part of Lean. Improvements are achieved through the untiring application of the main principles JIT and Jidoka. Chapter 5 is dedicated to describing improvement work.

In order to efficiently apply the two main principles JIT and Jidoka, the production flow must be sufficiently even or leveled. To this end, the description of JIT and Jidoka is preceded by a description of one of the most important conditions for achieving efficient flows, namely leveling.

Leveling

Leveling (or Heijunka in Japanese) is a cornerstone of Lean and it is crucial both from a flow and a quality perspective. Leveling means planning production to achieve a situation where the workload is, ideally, constant over time. This yields several positive effects such as improved conditions for:

- Efficiently applying the Lean principle Takt
- Maintaining steady and high quality levels
- Maintaining steady and high resource utilization

In order to efficiently apply the Lean principle Takt, the production volume per time unit should be leveled as much as possible. In a perfectly leveled flow, which cannot be fully achieved in practice, there are no stress peaks; the work pace is leveled and harmonic. A leveled workload also brings positive effects to quality. In addition, the absence of workload peaks provides ideal conditions for matching resources to the required capacity. Thus, we see that leveling helps sustain high levels of capacity utilization.

Considering these benefits, leveling of production should be one of the most important tasks in production planning, and it follows that to succeed in this task it is a good investment to maintain optimal conditions for production planning. Leveling is important in terms of volume as well as work content.

Leveling Production Volume

Leveling production volume simply means producing an equal number of units per time unit. Planning for the production of the same amount of product units per time unit will result in a leveled need for capacity. This in turn means that it is possible to dimension resources in the form of machines and people for a constant and known demand, which in turn provides the right conditions for achieving constant high capacity utilization. When the production volume differs from one day to the next, resources must be available to handle peaks in the workload. Some of these resources will be idle during non-peak times and this is of course a waste of resources.

Few (if any) organizations work in an environment where demand is constant, so total leveling is generally impossible. However, this should not be used as an excuse for not trying to level production. Every little step towards improved leveling will enhance conditions that will raise the operation's efficiency.

As an example, a company that produces to stock can generally vary stock sizes in order to level production. However, the leveling of production volume can also be achieved in make-to-order production. Here it is a question of artificial leveling. One option is to use the stock of unproduced orders as a buffer between customer demand and production flow.

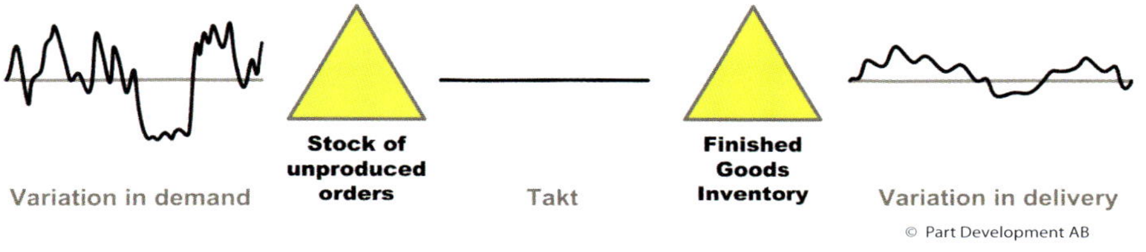

Figure 3-4. *Leveling production volume.*

When the agreed delivery times are sufficiently longer than the lead times, it may be possible to halt some orders so as to avoid overloading the production flow during high demand periods. This possibility is one of many reasons why it is important to reduce lead times. In a corresponding way it may be wise to advance production of some orders and thus fill otherwise empty production slots. In this way the workload in production is leveled, providing better conditions for matching capacity to the existing demand. Moreover, suppliers are provided with better conditions for producing parts and components cost-efficiently since their production can be leveled as well. All this is a consequence of improved leveling of consumption.

Leveling Production Volume ***Example***

A lunch restaurant achieved improved leveling by posting a chart showing actual variation in queuing times during lunch hours. Awareness of the large differences resulted in more and more customers changing their lunch times to avoid queuing. In this way the restaurant both achieved improved customer satisfaction and a more leveled workload for the staff.

Leveling Work Content

The other arena for leveling is work content. Many companies have a situation where they offer their customers several different products and/or variants that are produced in the same production flow. Normally, some of these products or product variants have more work content than others. To be able to utilize resources efficiently over time, variants with high work contents should be spread out as much as possible in the production sequence.

Figure 3-5. *The difference between a production sequence that is not leveled (top) and a production sequence that, given prevailing conditions, is as leveled as possible regarding work content (bottom).*

When many variants with high work contents are scheduled for consecutive production, the result is a large scale temporary increase of the workload. One obvious way to handle this situation is to add extra resources on those occasions when the workload is excessively high. This is an expensive solution if these extra resources cannot be used for other value-adding work at other times. If extra resources are not added, there will be congestion in the production flow which results in increased lead times for all products and variants.

Planning for products and variants with high work contents to be separated in the production sequence ensures good conditions for the handling of these variants without any excess capacity, or at least with less excess capacity.

As a rule, different products and variants have different bills of materials. Thus, an additional aspect of leveling of work content is that a better mix of the production sequence results in improved leveling of material consumption. This will in turn provide opportunities for improving the efficiency of the internal handling of materials, of external logistics, and of the suppliers' production.

In some cases it is wise to divide products and variants with common production flows and similarities in material consumption and work content into different product families with separate production flows for each product family. In this way the production flow within each product family is leveled.

© Part Development AB

Figure 3-6. *Different product families, with significant differences in work content and material consumption, that are produced in different production flows.*

Leveling Work Content — *Example*

The amount of resources required to process different orders in an order flow normally varies with the type of order. However, planning the operation so that orders with high work content are spread over the work hours as much as possible will level the workload for the resources involved. Another positive effect is that the variation in order lead time is reduced. This is because prolonged stops can be avoided when orders with high work content are not processed in one unbroken sequence.

Leveling work content in this way normally requires that there is a queue of unprocessed orders. To achieve sufficient distribution of orders having high work content there has to be a certain number of orders to choose from. In some cases the promised delivery time for an order may limit the possibilities of achieving desired leveling. Reducing lead time will therefore increase the possibilities of creating the desired order sequence. This is because it makes it easier to move an order forward or backward in time without exceeding the promised delivery time.

Leveling Production Volume and Work Content ***Example***

The time to perform a surgical operation depends on a number of factors such as the complexity of the operation. However, estimates of the approximate duration are usually available and may serve as the basis for planning operations.

Planning each work day so that large and small surgical operations alternate makes it possible to achieve operation sequences that maximize the utilization of the work hours. Apart from increasing capacity this will also increase the possibility of maintaining the number of surgical operations per day constant, i.e. a leveling of production volume. In addition, the workload within connected areas of healthcare, such as post-surgery wards and sterilization units, are leveled as well.

Leveling is an important condition for achieving efficient solutions within the main principles JIT and Jidoka. From this discussion, it is logical to extend the visual Lean model to also comprise leveling. Leveling is placed at the foundation of the temple to symbolize that it is important for the stability of the temple.

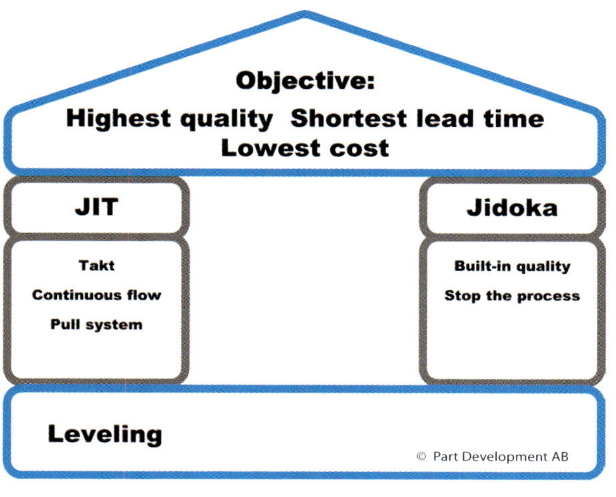

Figure 3-7. *Leveling is an important condition for JIT and Jidoka, and it is therefore visualized as a part of the foundation of the Lean model.*

Just-In-Time (JIT)

When we strive for Lean, we strive to produce and deliver at the right time, so we are neither in advance nor behind. The main principle Just-In-Time (JIT) is often rephrased as "the right parts in the right amounts at the right time". If everything was produced and delivered at exactly the right time, waste in the form of waiting time would be avoided. If all activities were to take place exactly when they should, the production flow would be totally predictable. This would in turn provide good conditions for reducing the inventory of purchased parts, buffers, and the finished goods inventory. In addition, the need for excess capacity would be avoided. This is the objective of the main principle JIT, which in turn comprises the principles:

- Takt
- Continuous flow
- Pull system

Takt

Takt is the Lean principle that sets the pulse in a production flow; it levels the rate of production. The term takt refers to the volume that should be produced per time unit. Thus, takt can be expressed as e.g. one per minute, 60 per hour, or 480 per shift. To be efficient, takt requires that the production flow is leveled - that equal amounts of products are produced in each time period.

In order to provide the members of the workforce with updated information on how the operation is progressing in relation to the takt, i.e. the customer demand, it is suitable to visualize this information. Figure 3-8 shows an example of how this kind of visualization can be made using an electronic information board. The board shows in real time how many acceptable products are produced (present value) as well as how many acceptable products should have been produced according to the current takt (target value). Thus, the difference between the present value and the target value represents the backlog.

Figure 3-8. *Example of visualization of operation progress relative the takt (customer demand). In this example the operation has fallen two products behind the takt.*

Takt can be broken down into takt time, i.e. the amount of time dedicated to each individual product in each process. This means that in a production flow with a 10 minute takt time, a product should leave each process step every 10 minutes. Thus, the production flow as a whole will produce one product every 10 minutes. Takt time is calculated as:

$$\textbf{Takt time} = \frac{\textbf{Planned production time}}{\textbf{takt}}$$

Planned production time is the time available for production within e.g. a shift. Thus, it is equal to the length of the shift minus planned breaks and those planned stops where it is known that nothing will be produced. The takt time is the time required to satisfy customer demand. It is calculated as the planned production time divided by the takt (i.e. the average customer demand rate). The difference between takt time and cycle time is that takt time is based on customer demand while cycle time is the result of technical conditions, i.e. the rate at which it is possible to produce.

There is a close connection between takt time and customer demand. However, in some types of operations such as projects and product development, it often occurs that customer demand cannot be easily expressed in numbers of units. In order not to devalue the term takt it would be better to use the term pulse to represent the follow-up of work progress versus plan. Thus, every follow-up (pulse) is a tuning between what is accomplished and what was planned.

Takt in itself has the advantage of having a leveling effect in the short term. We do not produce a smaller quantity in the morning and then have to be stressed in the afternoon so as to meet customer demand; Takt makes it possible to work at a constant rate during the entire work-day.

Takt time corresponds to the average demand rate given by the planned production time. Thus, the takt time is a breakdown of customer demand at the process level. In this way takt time indicates the time of delivery for each process step. This, in turn, provides the workforce with direct feedback on whether their delivery was on time or not. If a delivery to the next process step is not made on takt time, it is a deviation that will be noticed immediately.

With a takt time of one minute this confirmation is given once a minute. When takt time is visualized in real time, i.e. by visualization of the time remaining to the next takt, people have the possibility to continuously track their performance vis-à-vis takt time. An electronic board is one way of presenting takt time.

Figure 3-9. *Example of takt time visualization.*

It is important to emphasize that a clock, as shown in Figure 3-9, is only an example of the visualization of the principle Takt. In many cases Takt is applied in totally different ways. There are situations where Takt is not suitable to apply at the one-piece-level. However, Takt is in general more powerful the closer to the one-piece-level one gets. This because the frequent tuning of progress makes it easier to discover even the smallest deviations.

One of the fundamental aims of the principle Takt is to detect deviations. In practice it works like this: if a product has not left the production flow when the takt time is out, it is a sign that there is waste somewhere in the process. The takt time is important because small deviations would probably not have been discovered if the follow-up activities focused only on the number of products produced per shift. Even if they had been discovered, it would probably have been difficult to trace the root cause, i.e. the real cause.

Major instances of waste, such as machine and equipment breakdowns lasting several hours, are normally easy to discover also when the principle Takt is not applied. However, those small deviations that take place daily in all processes are definitely more difficult to detect. Nevertheless, discovering these small deviations is important, and the gain of solving many small deviations is substantial. Problem solving is normally quicker and generates more commitment when many small problems have to be dealt with rather than a few large ones.

The following example explains this statement. You and your colleague are competing about which one of you will first make $10 by picking up money from the street. You decide to pick up any coin you find, while your colleague will not bother to pick up anything less than a $10 bill. Which one of you do you think will get to $10 first?

Figure 3-10. *Many small coins can make a fortune.*

The Takt principle is applicable to any operation but its practical implementations must be adapted to prevailing circumstances. Here are some examples:

Takt in Automatic Processes *Example*

An automatic process where the cycle time is longer than the takt time will have problems in delivering unless extra resources are spent or overtime is added.

However, if the cycle time is shorter than the takt time, a choice exists between either running the equipment slower, to e.g. reduce wear, or to halt the equipment during a part of the takt time.

Short Takt Times *Example*

When producing small and simple products, it may be difficult to apply the Takt principle at the one-piece-level. This is because the takt time is so short that it may be difficult to track. In such cases it is preferable to reduce the resolution of the takt by applying Takt at the package unit level.

If the takt time per part is 6 seconds and there are 1000 parts per package unit, Takt can be applied by continuously tracking whether a package unit is delivered every 100 minutes. Also at this relatively coarse-grained level, Takt enables the discovery of considerably more deviations than if Takt had not been applied.

Long Takt Times *Example*

For products with large work contents and long cycle times it may be difficult to apply Takt at the product level as the takt time is so long that it masks deviations that occur during the work cycle. In these cases it is recommended that the resolution of the takt is increased by dividing the takt time into smaller time units.

For example, if the takt time per product is 8 hours, progress can be tuned e.g. once an hour. However, this requires that the work method is so well defined that there is a relevant reference to which progress can be tuned. Even at this relatively coarse-grained level Takt provides the necessary conditions for discovering deviations that would have remained hidden if Takt had not been applied at all.

Different Takt Times in Different Parts of the Production Flow

Example

In some cases takt time differs between different parts of the production flow. The formula for calculating takt time shows that there are two possible reasons for this. One reason is that different parts of the production flow have different demand rates. The other possible reason is that the planned production time differs between different departments along the production flow.

A company assembling a product variant also turns parts for this product. The machine workshop that turns the parts operates two shifts whereas assembly works a regular day shift. Each product contains three turned parts, and the machine workshop turns parts solely for this product variant. The demand rate for assembly is 16 products per day, which gives a demand rate for turned parts of 48 parts per day.

The formula for takt time calculation gives a takt time of 30 minutes for assembly (8 hours divided by 16 products). The same formula gives us a takt time of 20 minutes for the turning operation (16 hours divided by 48 parts).

Pulse in Projects

Example

An assignment that is limited in time, such as a project, should have a time schedule to clarify agreed deadlines. The time schedule reflects the customer demand and sets the pulse of the project, i.e. a kind of takt. The time schedule gives the time allotted to each activity. If the schedule is sufficiently detailed it can serve as the norm by which project progress is tuned.

Thus, applying pulse to a project means tuning project activity progress by referring to the time schedule as frequently as possible. Tuning meetings are sometimes denoted pulse meetings. In this way deviations can be discovered at an early stage. When the progress adjustment rate is raised, more and more deviations as well as smaller deviations can be detected. This is desirable as it normally makes problem-solving easier. In addition, frequent tuning of project progress makes it possible to take counter-measures early on, so that deviations from the time schedule can be minimized.

Moreover, management and control of an operation benefit from applying Takt or pulse. Leaders as well as employees need frequent and systematic information on how the operation progresses compared to plan. Management needs this information to be able to make the right decisions at the right time. For the workforce it is more a question of being provided with up-to-date information to be able to control the operation within their areas of responsibility. In addition, the organization needs to be aware of what deviations have been detected and thus have to be solved.

A way of working that supports this need is called "daily control". It is based on visualization and is a forum for frequent tuning of operational performance in relation to plan. The plan should in turn reflect customer demand. Thus daily control can be viewed as a systematic method of tuning the outcome with the takt or pulse.

15052007

Patient	Admission date	Plan of Care	Discharge planning	Planned discharge date	Status
Jones 78 ♀	10 May	11 May	~~14 May~~ 16 May	~~16 May~~ 18 May	Worsening condition
Smith 81 ♂	10 May	12 May	15 May	17 May	Plan to go home
Jackson 69 ♀	11 May	12 May	16 May	18 May	Awaiting test results

	9/2	10/2	11/2	12/2	13/2	Comment
Machining 1	1400/1400	1349/1400				Mtrl. shortage 10/2
Hardening	600/600	600/600				
Machining 2	200/200	220/220				
Assembly	34/76	73/73				Tool breakdown 9/12
Quality Control	64/64	62/63				Test prog. malfunct. 10/2
Shipping	210/210	210/210				

Figure 3-11. *Examples of boards for daily control within healthcare and manufacturing.*

With short daily meetings where the operational performance during the last 24 hours is compared to the target value, the entire organization can rapidly become aware of deviations. This in turn creates conditions for rapid actions. Another positive effect of daily control is that it normally results in decision makers becoming more aware of how the operation works, and what problems it faces every day. Daily control is an effective way to apply the basic thinking of the Lean principle Takt in controlling the operations.

Continuous Flow

The Lean principle Continuous Flow denotes striving to keep products and materials continuously moving. In practice, wholly continuous flows are not possible to achieve. However, one should *strive* for continuous flows by minimizing the number of stops as well as stoppage times. Every stop entails waiting time, and this waiting time is a form of waste. More stops necessitate longer lead times, which in turn imply decreased flexibility in meeting customer requirements as well as increased costs. Having products waiting to be processed also requires more space, which may be problematic.

In order to come closer to a continuous flow, and thereby reduce lead times, one should strive for:

- Short distances between process steps
- Small buffers
- Small package units
- Frequent transports

The layout of the production flow has a significant influence on the possibility of approaching continuous flow. In an effective layout the distance between process steps is short, which contributes to keeping waiting times between process steps short. Changing the layout in this direction often reduces waste more than does solely focusing on improving single processes by e.g. reducing processing time by a few minutes or seconds.

A buffer can be thought of as specially allotted storage space where Work In Progress (WIP) waits before being further processed. Work In Queue (WIQ) is actually a better expression since WIP is usually spent queuing. Buffering entails interruptions in the production flow, which extend lead times. Buffers are often necessary to compensate for various kinds of waste in the production flow, but they should be kept as small as possible. When attempting to achieve continuous flow it is therefore important to tackle the conditions and deviations causing a need for buffers. One example of a condition that creates a need for buffering is long change-over times. Long change-over times tend to increase batch sizes, which in turn will increase the need for buffering.

The number of parts in a package unit is a kind of batch sizing that is often overlooked. The size of the package unit creates a need for a buffer in the same way as the size of the batch. If, for example, there are 100 parts in a package unit, the first part will have to wait in the unit until part number 100 arrives. Reducing the size of the unit is one way to approach a continuous flow. Thus, approaching a continuous flow implies striving to reach batch sizes of one, i.e. one-piece-flow.

This effect of smaller package units will materialize only if transport frequency is increased. If the package size in the above example is reduced to 50 parts, there will be no effect on the production flow if the package units are not picked up more often. Ideally, parts should not need packaging at all within the production flow. Instead they should be rapidly transported to the next process step by e.g. a short conveyor belt.

The conditions for achieving continuous flow that have been described here are as valid for flows between factories as within factories. Long distances to suppliers are a drawback in the effort to achieve a continuous flow throughout the entire value stream. This because long distances tend to give rise to large buffers, large package units and low transport frequencies.

Continuous Flow ***Example***

In healthcare, where the flow comprises patients, short waiting times are of great importance. All stops in the flow mean extra waiting time for the patient and also longer lead time as well as increased waste. This may in turn entail extended suffering, extended sick leave without income, more contacts with healthcare to find out the current position in the waiting queue, etc. The waiting time also entails an increased workload for the healthcare organization due to more questions. In addition, some patients' health may deteriorate while awaiting treatment. These negative effects create an unnecessary workload for the personnel. This is often denoted false customer demand. Striving to achieve a continuous flow by organizing so that the flow of patients is put in focus, rather than solely the efficiency of specific processes, will produce opportunities to reduce waiting time in the flow.

Transport Frequency *Example*

In administrative flows, increased transport frequency may concern part deliveries. In a typical administrative flow, there are a number of resources that refine information in process steps. Delivering information in as small units as possible, instead of waiting to pass on all information until everything is finished, will reduce the time spent in the flow by the administrative product. This is a cheap, rapid and often completely uncontroversial way of taking steps towards a continuous flow in an administrative operation. It does not entail much of a change for the staff as the ways of working and the work pace remain unchanged. The only difference is that the actual delivery is different and this may bring significant positive effects to the flow as a whole.

Pull System

The third principle under the main principle JIT pertains to how processes in a production flow should be controlled. A pull system is characterized by production being triggered by a demand signal from a subsequent process. Thus, it can be said that the information flow and the physical flow run in parallel. The last process in the production flow, i.e. the process that is in contact with the customer, receives a customer order and starts processing. This results in the need for deliveries from the upstream process. In this way the demand signal is propagated stepwise upstream in the production flow.

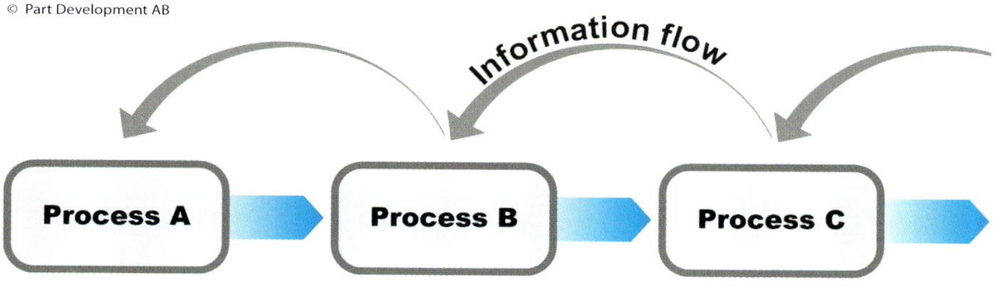

Figure 3-12. *The Pull system principle means that the customer process sends information on current demand upstream.*

A major benefit of the pull system is that the demand signal that is sent upstream considers not only the actual customer demand at product level but also any deviations that may have occurred. If one of the processes in the production flow stops, it will not consume anything. This implies that it will not signal demand to its supplying process. Thus, the supplying process will stop due to lack of orders. In this way undesired buffers caused by production disturbances can be avoided.

Kanban is a simple method to pass demand signals between processes. Kanban is a Japanese word that means card or visual evidence. A simplified explanation of Kanban is that a person working in one process along the flow calls for parts that have been produced in a preceding process. When the parts are collected, a signal (Kanban) is left behind. This is a signal to the preceding process to refill and start production of the product variant and in the quantity stated by the Kanban. Thus, the function of Kanban is similar to a reorder point system or to a buffer control. In these cases it is instead a defined buffer level that signals what, when and how much should be produced.

Kanban as a control method is simple and supports the Lean principle Pull system. However, it is important to emphasize that it is not always effective. To reap the full benefits of Kanban the prevailing conditions should be characterized by:

- High and leveled demand
- Short replenishment times
- Small (physical) parts

Using Kanban does not have to imply that cards must be used to signal demand. The signal may as well take the form of an empty package unit, a mark on the floor, or a light signal.

Pull System *Example*

An order flow may consist of a number of resources delivering to each other to complete a customer order. Each resource has a defined capacity in terms of how many orders can be processed per time unit. The number of orders being loaded into the flow should be adapted to this capacity.

In a flow of this kind, it is possible to define permitted levels in each inbox, i.e. in the buffer in front of each resource. It may e.g. be expressed as a maximum number of waiting, unprocessed orders. Thus, there is an agreement between each pair of resources in the flow. When each resource has updated information on its internal customer's (next resource in the flow) inbox, a pull system can be established. When a customer's inbox is filled with orders up to a defined maximum level, it should be considered full and no more orders should then be passed on until the inbox has returned to the desired level, i.e. until the receiver is ready to receive it. This will highlight deviations in specific parts of the flow. Members of the workforce who also deliver to other resources may change their work order according to current demand.

Pull system does not necessarily mean that the demand signal is transferred stepwise between the process steps as in Figure 3-12. Sometimes it may be necessary to leapfrog some processes due to the necessity to reduce lead times or that there is a wide range of variants, at the same time as product design entails that the customer order point is placed at a process early in the product flow. Although a demand signal omits some process steps, it is still to some extent a pull system. It should be emphasized that in this case it is even more important to ensure that FIFO (First In, First Out) is applied. FIFO means that all products leave the flow in the same order as they entered the flow.

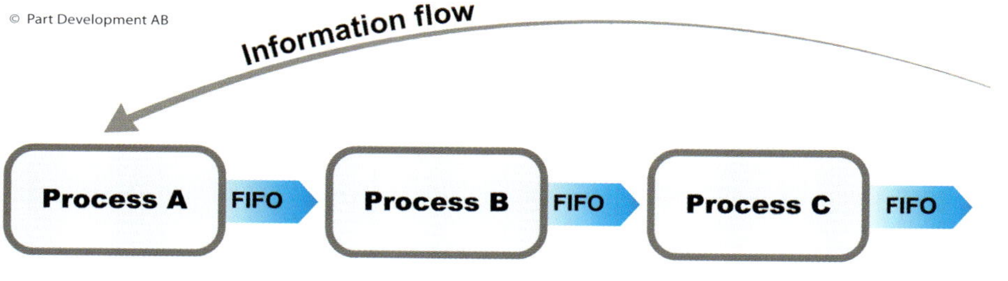

Figure 3-13. *Example of the Pull system principle, where the information flow omits some processes.*

Pull system provides conditions for using available capacity to produce the correct products, i.e. the products that the customers demand at that particular point in time. Thus, pull system means producing the right products at the right time as seen from a customer demand perspective. By avoiding producing "wrong" products, delivery reliability of the production flow will increase.

The opposite of pull system is called push system. In a push system, the signal to start production comes from the master schedule. It means that production orders are distributed based on how the orders were originally planned to be produced in terms of product variant, quantity and start of production.

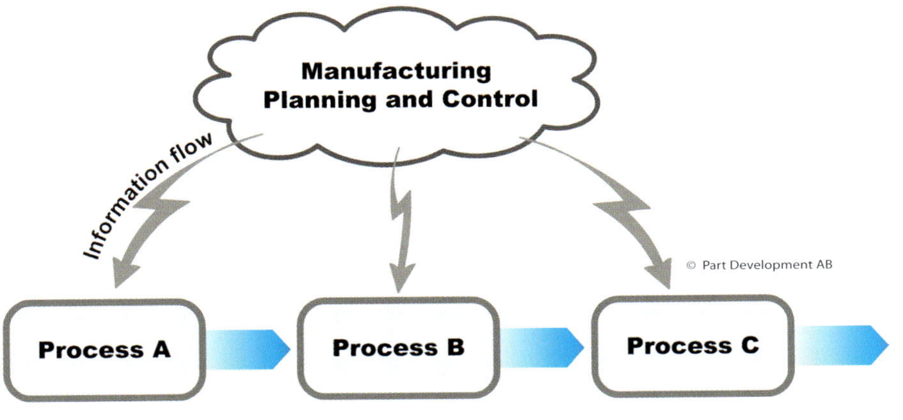

Figure 3-14. *In a push system the information flow is independent of the physical flow until the next re-planning.*

The orders are often distributed via the company's MPC system (Manufacturing Planning and Control). This means that the push system does not take into account unexpected occurrences but is solely based on the schedule. In some cases this schedule, in turn, is based on forecasted information thus increasing the risk that wrong products are produced at the wrong time. Thus, the main problem with the push system is that it does not take sufficient account of changes in customer demand, production disturbances, etc. that occur in the short term. It is like driving a car and not looking at the road but only at the map, i.e. missing a lot of important information from the surrounding traffic.

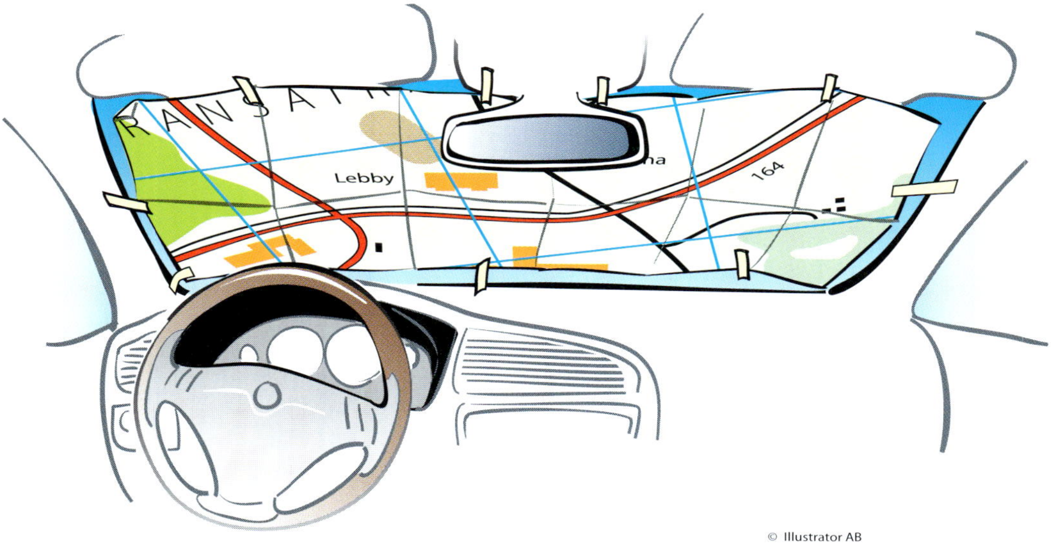

Figure 3-15. *Driving a car without taking unexpected occurrences (deviations) into consideration will not take you safely to your destination.*

Jidoka

The right-hand pillar in the Toyota Production System (TPS) represents the main principle Jidoka. This is a Japanese term meaning to build quality into the product by ensuring that everything is done correctly from the start and that a process is halted if something still turns out to be wrong. Thus, it concerns achieving predictability in product quality. The main principle Jidoka consists of the principles:

- Built-in quality
- Stop the process

Built-in Quality

The most important condition for achieving a high-quality process is that every member of the workforce has the appropriate competence and complies with agreed ways of working. This will put the principle

Built-in quality into practice. In an automatic process there is often the possibility to correct the process automatically in order to continuously ensure high quality.

Building quality into a product is the opposite of the passive approach to quality, where quality is inspected into the product. The latter procedure has been, and still is to some extent, common. It is done by examining products for defects at specific quality inspection stations in order to determine if the products should be accepted or not. These quality inspection stations are still often present also in companies that have come a fair bit on their journey towards Lean. However, these companies have reduced their use of these quality inspections. In some cases they are only used for a few sample tests.

The effort to get it right from the start can be facilitated at the operational level by clarifying who the customer is. For example, a preassembly has a certain assembly station as its customer. From a quality point of view it is important that every member of the workforce is aware of who their internal customer is, i.e. the next process step in the value stream. It is also beneficial if the internal customer and the internal supplier are placed physically close to each other so that the relationship between the customer and the supplier is strengthened. This will facilitate and encourage real-time quality feedback, which in turn builds and strengthens the sense of responsibility.

Poka Yoke is a Japanese term meaning solutions that make it more or less impossible to get things wrong. It may e.g. be making the geometrical shape of a part so that it will be impossible to install it in the wrong way.

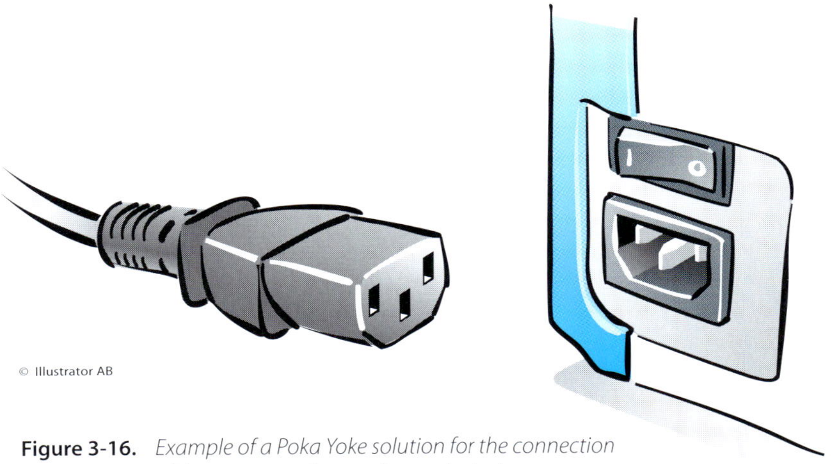

Figure 3-16. *Example of a Poka Yoke solution for the connection of the power cord to an electronic device.*

Solutions like this one are obviously desirable but difficult to apply in work methodology. An easier approach to "get it right from the start" would be to make getting-it-right easy. It must be assumed that all members of the workforce are doing their best. The question then is: how are they supported in this effort by work methodology, workplace layout, production flow layout, etc.? For example, is the material presented to the assembly operator in such a way that it is easy to choose the right part for a certain product variant?

Built-In Quality ***Example***

Built-in quality takes on another dimension in healthcare where mistakes can result in injuries or even deaths. For example, of the medicines available at a nursing ward some are completely harmless while others are very dangerous when administered wrongly. The packages of these medicines are often similar and they are handled in a stressful environment. In this case it is of extra importance to create the right conditions for making it easy to choose the right medicine. This may be facilitated by having different shapes and designs on the packages as well as on the product, separated storage, or different work procedures.

It is not unusual that the effort to improve efficiency at the workplace makes it more difficult to produce the right quality from the start. One common example is the goal to minimize the distance (number of steps) an assembly operator has to walk. From an efficiency perspective it may be preferable to standardize a work procedure in which the assembly operator collects all the parts at once, places the bolts used to fasten all parts to the product and finally tightens all the bolts. Such a set-up minimizes walking, but there is instead the risk that the assembly operator forgets to tighten some of the bolts. It would have been easier to get it right from the start by designing a way of working that enables the assembly operator to pick up one part at a time and immediately place and tighten the bolts for that part. Thus, in designing procedures there may be a trade-off between efficiency and product quality. Quality should have the highest priority as it has direct implications for the customer. In addition, high and consistent quality is a prerequisite for a highly efficient production flow.

Stop the Process

The Lean principle Stop the process means that a process or equipment should be halted immediately when a fault is discovered. Automated equipment that is automatically halted when something goes wrong provides the right conditions for high quality as well as high productivity. The fact that the equipment will not pass on any defects ensures quality. Another positive effect is that when the operator does not constantly have to supervise the equipment other tasks can be carried out in parallel. This improves the operator's productivity.

Stopping the process when something is wrong is of course also important in manual processes. The organization is forced to concentrate on quality problems before production is restarted. It may not be possible to solve the problem immediately in a manner that precludes the fault from recurring, but before production is restarted at least a short-term solution should be in place to ensure that defects cannot be propagated in the production flow. A temporary manual quality check is an example of a possible short-term solution.

If a process is not stopped when a fault is discovered, there is a risk that the same defect will appear on multiple products. As every member of the workforce knows that production time is valuable there is a risk that some of them will not dare to stop the process when needed. It is therefore important that management makes it clear to the whole workforce that everyone has the authority, and the obligation, to stop the process when something goes wrong. Such action must be constantly encouraged. Loss of production time is a considerably smaller waste than allowing quality defects to be passed on in the production flow. Stopping the process also contributes to make the problems visible to everyone, and it sends the signal that the problem must be solved quickly.

Stop the Process ***Example***

Stopping the process when something is wrong is of course equally important in non-manufacturing operations. It normally requires a lot of work to cope with faults that are passed on in the flow. Incorrect input into an information system may serve as an example. It may be difficult to recover all incorrect data and to be certain that nothing has been overlooked.

In healthcare there is a risk that faults create unnecessary suffering for the patient and that they also generate additional need for medical care as a result of the faulty treatment.

Relationships between the Principles

Each of the Lean principles is important to attain desired results in the Lean commitment. However, to be able to rank activities according to their importance, it is required to understand the relationships between the principles. Figure 3-17 illustrates the relationships between leveling, JIT and Jidoka. The latter two are main principles while leveling is not, but leveling is an important condition for JIT as well as for Jidoka.

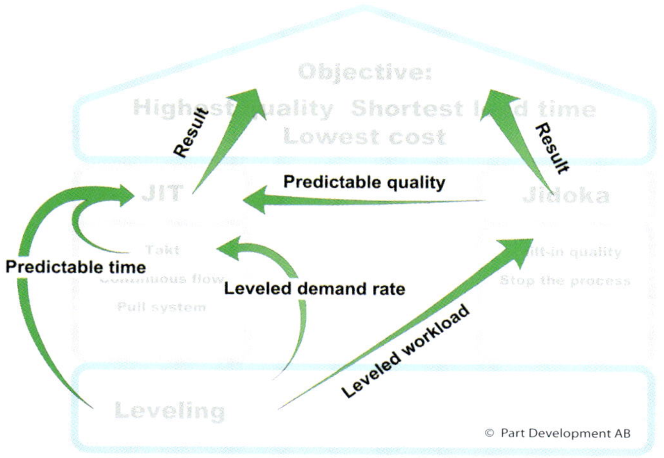

Figure 3-17. *Relationships between leveling and the Lean principles.*

It should be mentioned that in addition to leveling, standardization is a basic condition for every successful Lean commitment. What standardization means and how it is related to the Lean principles is described in Chapter 4.

Leveling provides opportunities for producing the same quantities every day, and this in turn is a condition for applying Takt efficiently. Takt time is based on a certain demand rate and certain work hours. The takt time may be changed in the longer term but frequent changes in takt time should be avoided. If takt time is changed too frequently, there is a risk that the organization will get confused. Normally, changing takt time also implies that the production flow has to be rebalanced, which requires much work and at the same time new waste is normally introduced into the production flow. Eliminating this "new" waste is very time consuming.

Both leveling and Takt contribute to increased predictability in delivery times for each process in the production flow. Leveling a flow means leveling the workload of the production flow so that temporary queues are avoided. In this way leveling contributes to bringing predictability to product lead times. Takt in turn contributes to predictable lead times by reducing variations in process time. In a production flow where Takt is applied the product is always delivered at takt time unless unplanned stops in the process have occurred.

Leveling also supports the Lean principle Built-in quality. Periods of very high workloads often result in stress which may have a negative impact on product quality. Periods of underload have turned out to have negative effects on product quality as well. This because it is easy to let the mind wander from the work at hand when this work is not sufficiently stimulating. Leveling therefore contributes to improved and more predictable product quality by eliminating these sources of stress. It is well known that high quality has a positive effect on the financial result. An organization with a high and stable product quality is able to uphold better prices for their products at the same time as the internal costs for dealing with poor quality can be minimized.

At the end of the day, the main principle JIT is about creating efficient production flows. A necessary condition for this to succeed is that the processes in the production flow are predictable, i.e. that variation in production time as well as in quality is low. When each process in a production flow delivers on time with the right quality, it is possible to reduce buffers. This will reduce waste in a number of ways as the need for buffers between the processes of a production flow is partly the result of the need to have insurance against unforeseen occurrences. This need for insurance is reduced when the processes are predictable.

The creation of effective and efficient flows is necessary to achieve the overall goals of an operation such as high quality, short lead time and low cost. The organization that is successful in this work will have a strong position in price negotiations with their customers and costs can be kept low. Consequently the financial result is improved. This discussion about effective and efficient production flows is valid for supply chains within a department as well as between companies.

Create Own Solutions

The principles of the Toyota Production System (TPS) represent ways of thinking. They provide support and guidance for how to relate to various issues. Unfortunately, organizations often study other organizations that are successful with Lean, copy the successful solutions and apply them in their own operations. It is easy to be impressed by other companies' achievements at seminars and company visits. However, the problem is that what can be seen at a visit are other organizations' solutions to their specific problems given their specific conditions. It is far from certain that these solutions will work in another organization. The reason is, of course, that the thoughts behind the solutions cannot be copied.

Often it is the way that the solutions were created that makes them work in practice. An existing solution that works in one organization may not work at all in another, even though the principles behind the solution are the same. This because different organizations have different conditions. Even if a copied solution would work, a small change in the prevailing conditions could have unexpected effects. For example, when it is not understood why a production flow is dimensioned in a certain way it will be difficult to adapt that flow to new conditions.

Figure 3-18. *Example of what could happen when a way of working is copied without considering differences in conditions.*

Increasing knowledge about Lean is important. However, to be successful with a Lean commitment, the application of the Lean principles has to be done at Genba. The operation's own unique conditions prevail at the workplace, where value is created. The conditions may be physical as well as mental, and these conditions together with the Lean principles should provide the operation's *own* solutions to its *own* problems.

Toyota is a good example. It would be impossible for a Western company to find success by copying how Toyota works today. The reason for this is that Toyota's present way of working has evolved through continuous improvements since the 1950's. Every organization has to start from where it is and think about how it can take the next small step towards Lean.

The Principles Support Long-term Efficiency

The purpose of the Lean principles is to eliminate waste. Eliminating waste is a long-term and continuous effort in all organizations striving for Lean.

Outside the framework of the Lean principles there may be solutions to problems bringing higher efficiency in the short term, but they are usually apt to be replaced by Lean solutions in the longer term. This because solutions aligned with the Lean principles to a greater extent highlight the waste that can really be eliminated. Balancing the solutions in this way requires a proper understanding of the Lean principles.

Techniques like Discrete Event Simulation (DES) are often used to evaluate competing alternatives. The problem with these kinds of evaluations is that they evaluate static performance, i.e. they do not consider the potential of the improvements that can be made when waste is highlighted. This potential for improvement is overlooked in Discrete Event Simulations.

The following example illustrates this statement. A company is about to decide whether to introduce Takt to their assembly operations or not. If their choice is based solely on calculations or simulations they will most likely conclude that an assembly system without Takt is the most efficient alternative. The reason is that the Takt principle does not allow assembly at a faster rate than at takt time. The result is that every minute of an unplanned stop is time that is forever lost. In an assembly system without Takt, there is always the possibility of catching up lost production time by running the operations a bit faster than normal. In this way, lost production can be retrieved within normal work hours. Thus, a minute's stop will have less serious consequences in a non-Takt assembly system.

The message is that a traditional analysis will probably come to the conclusion that an assembly system without Takt is the most efficient alternative. However, with proper understanding of the Lean principles, the conclusion may very well be the opposite. When introducing Takt to the assembly system, deviations in the form of stops, faults, etc. will be highlighted. No one can ignore a problem that halts the entire assembly system. Hence the organization becomes aware of the waste and it can often be eliminated by small and simple means. When this improvement work is allowed to prosper, the original assembly time can be considerably reduced with increased efficiency as a result. The price that may have to be paid is an initial decrease in efficiency, but in an organization with a functioning improvement plan it should not take too long before efficiency is raised beyond that of the assembly system without Takt. In the long run, a production flow with Takt is usually unbeatable.

Managing through Principles

Management in an organization striving for Lean should focus on training the employees in understanding and applying Lean principles in their daily work. The manager is the teacher and the authority of the manager is largely provided by his/her Lean knowledge. For this reason managers at Toyota undergo long operational training programs where they learn to apply the Lean principles before they take up their new positions.

At Toyota in Japan, managers work their way to the top through many years of operational duty, from the shop floor and up. In this way they have come to understand the Lean principles through practical training in everyday work. Contrary to Toyota in Japan, managers at Toyota in the US are often recruited from other companies. Managers entering Toyota in this way undergo many months of training led by a Japanese mentor. The training is practical in nature and concerns working with the details of the ongoing operations. This is very different from the management training programs that managers in Western companies normally undergo in preparation for their new positions.

Management effectiveness in Lean is based on training the workforce so that they think in terms of improvements and take own initiatives. Having a proper understanding of the Lean principles, members of the workforce are able to find their own solutions to the problems they are faced with. The manager can feel secure when delegating, as the principles provide a framework for what is desirable and acceptable. In an organization that has come far on its journey towards Lean, every member of the workforce is his/her own process developer and problem solver. Of course they will still need support, but this would be from experts to help them solve complicated problems rather than from managers controlling every detail.

Inevitably, situations will emerge that will cause the workforce to question the Lean principles. This usually happens when faced with a specific problem. It may for instance be in situations where shortcuts are considered to be more efficient and Lean principles are considered to lead to solutions that are substantially more complex or expensive. On these occasions, management presence is of utmost importance. The manager should be able to instantly seize this golden opportunity for training the workforce in understanding the principles. The way management handles these kinds of situations determines to what extent the workforce will actually accept the Lean principles.

In some situations it may be wise to deviate from Lean principles, but such beneficial deviations will usually not be performed in organizations where there is a lack of understanding leading to an all too orthodox application of the principles. This is probably one of the reasons why some people find these principles hard to accept. When it is deemed that a better solution exists outside the Lean framework, it is important to first make an appropriate analysis so that everyone will understand *why* the deviation from a certain Lean principle is taken. Common sense is always good but in combination with a proper analysis it is even better.

Methods – Ways of Doing

The Lean principles are important in that they guide the employees' way of *thinking* and put people on the path to solutions that lead to Lean. However, thinking alone is not enough to make a difference for practical matters, methods are needed for this: methods are ways of *doing*.

There are a number of methods that in one way or another support Lean, and some of them are described in the appendix. However, the relationships between the principles and the methods should first be explained. Understanding the difference between principles and methods is an important prerequisite to being able to develop operations in the right direction.

A Lean principle is a way of thinking that is always usable. In order to be generally usable and applicable it should be vaguely formulated and not exert too much control. The principle should indicate the *what* but not the *how*. In organizations that have come far on their journey towards Lean, the principles are often used as check points to make sure that nothing has been forgotten or misinterpreted. Applying the principles one by one and questioning whether the suggested solution is supported by the principle represents a kind of quality assurance from a Lean perspective. At the same time it forces important discussions to be taken on how the Lean principles should be interpreted.

In contrast to a principle, a method indicates how something should be done: a method indicates or describes a way of doing or working. A method is what makes an impact in reality and what creates results. Methods can of course be company specific, but common methods are normally satisfactory. The connection between principles and methods is that the principles provide guidance in choosing the right method from the wide range of methods available.

The choice of method should be preceded by a thorough analysis. That a method is classified as a Lean method does not necessarily mean it will improve operations. It would be like claiming that an excellent toolboard would turn anyone into a skilled mechanic.

Figure 3-19. *It is not the tools that make the skilled mechanic.*

Methods as a Means of Control

In traditional organizations results are the incentives used by management to lead the organization in the desired direction. These companies are characterized by their focus on key performance indicators and measurable goals, which most often have a direct financial connection. Further, individuals in the organization have great freedom to find their own solutions and to do things their own way. Management is rarely interested in *how* the work is done, instead what matters is that the measurable result is acceptable. The details that make up the entirety of the operations are left to the workforce, while management focuses on staking out new directions (sometimes all too often for the organization to be able to keep up with) and surveying the results at an aggregated level. When management is dissatisfied it is not unusual that a new drive is launched to make a radical change. At the same time the workforce becomes increasingly confused when given a set of new directives once again.

Management by Results	Management by Means
Management focus on measurable results	The right result will come when the right methods are applied
Decisions controlled by KPI results	Results are consequences of chosen methods and how they are applied
How the operation is run is not the most important issue	Results are continuously tracked to make sure that the chosen methods bring the desired results
Management focus is primarily on the aggregate level	Focus is on working with the details
Managers ask for results	Managers ask for ways of working

Figure 3-20. *Management by Results as opposed to Management by Means.*

Results are of course also extremely important in an organization that is striving for Lean. The difference lies in how results are approached. An organization striving for Lean generally has more of a long-term approach than traditional organizations. Good results are required to survive in the long term, but in the short term focus should instead be put on the ways of working, i.e. how the work is done. This applies both to workforce and to management even when the company is acting in an environment that demands excellent financial results every quarter.

Basing itself on Lean principles the organization picks ways of working (i.e. methods) that are expected to yield the desired results. When this choice is made, training and use of these methods should have top priority for the workforce as well as the management. There is a conviction that the chosen methods will yield the right results if they are correctly applied. The suitability of the methods is continuously evaluated, but the methods are not changed lightly, but are rather altered only after thorough analysis. When the result is not satisfactory, the first question to ask should be whether the method has been correctly used. If this is the case and if at the same time it is evident that the wrong method was chosen, a new method should be chosen with guidance from the Lean principles. This way of managing an enterprise is called Management by Means.

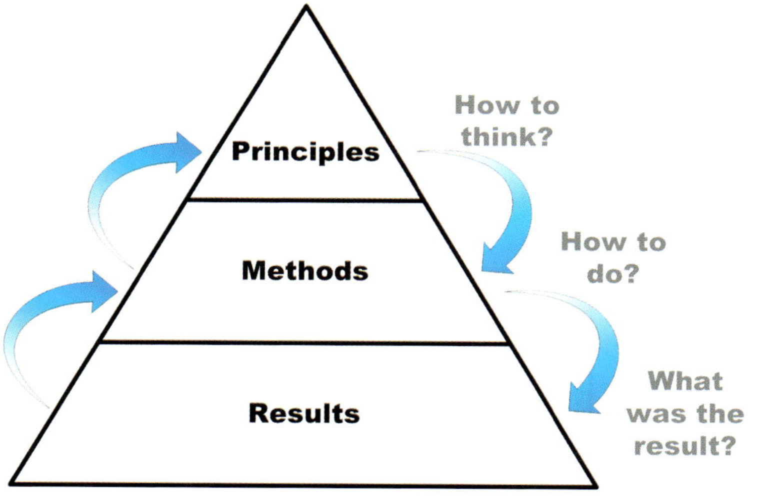

Figure 3-21. *Relationships between principles, methods, and results.*

The pyramid in Figure 3-21 symbolizes the idea that a small number of Lean principles support a great number of disparate methods (ways of working). The results from these ways of working impact a very large number of result parameters in every area where operations are performed.

Management by Means is based on the belief that evolution in small and controlled steps is more successful in the long term than is revolution. Here revolution is taken to mean large and drastic changes brought about in a short period of time. At the outset Westerners, who at school as well as in business are brought up to focus on results, may be frustrated as it takes such a long time to reach their goals. This even though slow and controlled changes have a better chance of survival in the long run.

Organizations that are in a hurry and revolutionize their operations using large and rapid changes are apt to fall back to earlier ways of working. The ways of working are changed to be “more Lean” while management continues to demand short-term results and shows no interest in how the new ways of working actually support daily operations. In the end the members of the workforce become confused and easily fall back to their original ways of working as “that appears to be what the managers appreciate the most”. Thus, successful Management by Means is primarily about active and supporting leadership as opposed to controlling leadership. Belief in the methods chosen, endurance, interest in operations and the ability to put the right questions to the workforce are important cornerstones.

If it's not defined what is normal - How is it possible to see that something is NOT normal?

4. Stan

Standardization – Reveals Waste

Lean principles form the foundation of an organization's development towards Lean. The principles act as a guide to concrete solutions in operations. These solutions must be formalized and distributed to those concerned, usually in the form of agreements on the details of how the operations should be run. An agreement of this kind is called a standard.

A standard is a description of the best currently known and accepted way to perform a task, store material, control production, etc. In this way every standard is a concrete and agreed application of Lean principles. The standard is valid until a new and better solution has been agreed upon, at which point this new solution becomes the standard. In this way a standard within Lean can, and should, be changed whenever necessary.

Standardization is important at the production flow level as well as at the process level. Everything that affects an operation's stakeholders, i.e. customers, workforce, owners and society, needs to be standardized. Standardized WIP levels are an example of standardization that is relevant at the production flow level.

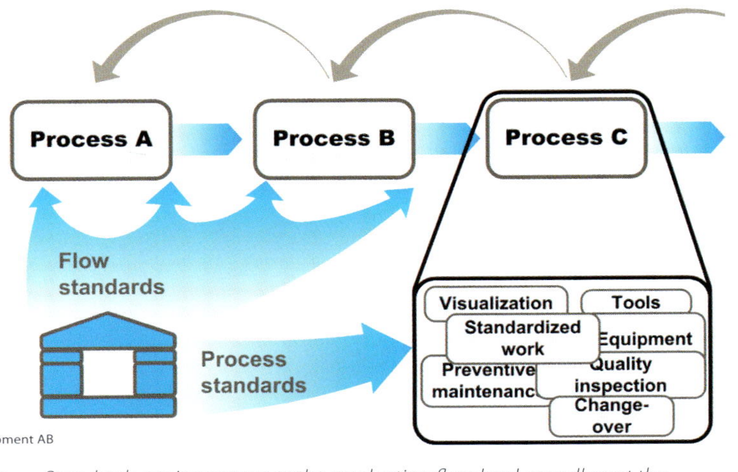

Figure 4-1. *Standards are important at the production flow level as well as at the process level. The solutions that are standardized should be based on the Lean principles.*

The Term Standardization

All that has been standardized is not necessarily the best, or even good, but quite simply that on which there is currently an agreement. This agreement lies at the heart of standardization. The standard should be the natural starting point of all activities and standardization is above all important in:

- Detecting deviations
- Contributing to predictability
- Creating knowledge

When there is an agreement over where goods should be stored, how demands should be communicated, how many parts there should be in a package unit, etc., then detecting deviations from this agreement is feasible. In contrast, if specifications, work methods, etc. have not been defined, how can one claim that something is a deviation? Thus, standardization is the basis that makes it possible to detect deviations, which in turn is a necessity if waste is to be eliminated.

Where there is no standard, problems will not be identifiable. Measured results may indicate that there are problems in the operation but it will be difficult to pinpoint the cause when there are no rights and wrongs. When, for example, it is not defined under what circumstances a process in a value stream should be stopped, no one can call into question why the process storage space is overfull and why the workers have started piling materials in the truck corridor. By the same token, it is difficult to question why one member of the workforce performs a task in two hours while another can do it in 30 minutes.

Figure 4-2. *The absence of standards makes life troublesome.*

In an operation where everything is done in the agreed manner, an environment that provides conditions for achieving predictable results is in place. Predictability is a central concept in Lean due to its great importance in terms of waste elimination from value streams. As an example, a value stream consisting exclusively of totally predictable processes will normally require significantly smaller buffers than value streams with unpredictable processes. Unpredictability implies insecurity that calls for some kind of insurance. Insurance in this context is often provided by larger buffers.

A standard describes the best currently known, formalized and agreed upon way to e.g. perform an activity. Propagating standards in the organization also means that knowledge is spread which in turn contributes to learning. By consistently sticking to standards all members of the workforce share the best knowledge currently known. In addition, some of the deviations that surface when the organization is working according to standard will reveal a need for competence development. In this way the need for learning will become apparent and can be dealt with through education and training of the individuals needing it. Other types of deviations will reveal problems and shortcomings in the operations that would probably not have been detected without standardization, at least not as consistently. There may be problems in processes as well as in flows. Being aware of these problems will, in itself, increase knowledge about how the operation is working at the detail level.

Basically there is nothing that cannot be standardized, but what is relevant to standardize may differ from operation to operation. However, standardized work, i.e. the standardization of manual work, is more or less applicable to all operations. Therefore, the remainder of this chapter will focus on standardized work.

Standardized Work

A standard for manual work is called standardized work. Standardized work comprises all the manual activities in the process producing the product. However, it does not describe the product itself. Instead, the product is defined and described by the design data, which may be viewed as a product standard. However, the design of the product influences the content of the standardized work.

There are, above all, three reasons why standardized work is important in an operation:

- Safety/ergonomics
- Quality
- Efficiency

Workplace safety and ways of working that are designed in such a way that good ergonomics are achieved should always have top priority in all operations. No one should have to risk his/her life or health at work. Thus, by standardizing a certain way of working, an agreement is made on how safety and ergonomics should be handled in daily operations. It may e.g. concern the use of lifting aids that might slow down work but are important from an ergonomic point of view. When the use of a certain lifting aid is standardized no one needs to feel that its use is a waste of time. In this way, the conditions that allow work to be done in a safe and ergonomically sound way are improved.

Applying standardized work creates conditions for making everyone work in the same manner. This contributes to stable product quality. However, if the standardized work is inadequate this stable quality does not necessarily mean high quality. From an improvement perspective stability, i.e. reduced variation, is very important. If a certain quality problem occurs time after time it implies a systematic problem which is normally somewhat easier to tackle than problems that are more random in nature. Having an effective improvement work enables systematic attacks on the weaknesses in the standardized work, and root causes are eliminated at the same pace as the standardized work is improved.

Another reason to apply standardized work is to increase process efficiency. The standardized work describes the best currently known and agreed way to perform a certain activity. This specific way of working consumes a certain amount of time. The established normal time consumption is a necessary part of the standardized work. When the standardized work is known to take a certain amount of time it is possible to detect time deviations, i.e. deviations in the form of activities that take too long or too short time. From an improvement perspective, it is important that these types of deviations are detected so that the conditions for performing the work according to correct time scales can be improved.

If everyone performing a certain task does it in the best known way, efficiency should be better than if everyone does it their own way. Of course, this does not mean that people should stop thinking for themselves, quite the opposite. The standardized work creates opportunities to implement all the good ideas that exist in the organization, and to make sure that they are communicated to everyone. If one person comes up with a brilliant idea, it would be a pity if this idea was not forwarded to others. Standardized work is a very effective tool in communicating this kind of knowledge.

When different people use different ways of working they will probably consume different amounts of time. This is a problem when e.g. creating a balanced production flow, as capacity is dependent on who is performing a certain task at a certain point in time. However, even if everyone works in the same way it does not guarantee exactly the same time for everyone. We all have different abilities and aptitudes that we bring to our work, but if everyone works in the same standardized manner the differences will be smaller. To achieve really good results, everyone must be trained to accomplish their tasks in the shortest possible repeatable time.

In operations of a less repetitive nature than a typical manufacturing process, it is often difficult to get agreement for applying standardized work. This may be the case in e.g. operations requiring a large amount of creativity. Another problem often highlighted is that it must be possible to adapt the operation to unforeseeable circumstances. One might for example run up against rusted stuck screws when servicing a relatively new car, or find something unexpected during a surgical operation. Work tasks that are creative in nature or difficult to envisage do not imply that standardization can be brushed aside. All operations, no matter how creative or unpredictable, include a large amount of repetitive activities. It is not unusual that considerably more than half of the work time is spent on repetitive activities. It is this repetitive work and not the creative part that should first be standardized. Executing repetitive activities in the best known way will improve efficiency. In addition, more time can be spent on elements that add the most customer value and that are also most interesting to perform.

As long as a work task or a flow is not perfect it can be improved, and it is a well-known fact that perfect work tasks or flows do not exist in real life. In order to improve quality, time and cost it is important that the variation in work performance is minimal. This is a prerequisite to being able to make systematic improvements. For a customer in a service flow or a patient in a healthcare flow, customer satisfaction should be independent of who is carrying out the service or the medical care. Standardization reduces individual variations and the consistent application of standardized work within non-manufacturing operations brings benefits such as:

- Reduced vulnerability and increased predictability
- Reduced variation in quality
- Increased capacity

Reduced vulnerability means that knowledge on how work should be performed does not stay exclusively with certain specific individuals. This is important for being able to deal correctly with e.g. absences. Standardized work implies that much of the practical knowledge about how tasks should be executed is documented. This does not mean of course that everyone should be able to carry out work tasks without having the proper level of competence and training. Surgery should still be carried out by an experienced surgeon but not necessarily by exactly the same surgeon every time. The result in terms of quality and time should still be predictable.

Applying standardized work reduces the risk of forgetting and making mistakes. This contributes to reducing quality variation and results in a more predictable level of quality. This is why aviation pilots use checklists before every takeoff and landing although they often fly the same aircraft several times per day. They view checklists as an aid to achieve high and predictable quality, and the passengers appreciate this effort. Similarly, people in the service sector can use standardized work to provide customers with services of the same level of quality regardless of which individual is currently providing the service.

When all members of the workforce apply the same standardized work, it is possible to balance the workload between individuals. This prevents some people from being overloaded while others are underloaded. This is a common problem in administrative operations where the employees are organized based on customer regions. In these operations it is natural that the number of errands differs over time within each region and also between the regions. Without a standardized work procedure, e.g. where and how to file documents, it is difficult for colleagues from different customer regions to support each other when workloads peak. However, if there were a common set of standards for all customer regions, capacity could be increased at the same time as the workload for each employee would be leveled.

Standardizing Work

The optimum way to produce a standard supporting daily operations is to allow the members of the workforce to produce it themselves. This will:

- Facilitate the approval process
- Ensure the correct level of detail
- Ensure simplicity
- Facilitate the process of "getting it right"

Standardized work created by someone outside the process, e.g. a manager or some outside "expert", is often met with skepticism by those who will perform the work. This is because the actual expertise on how to perform the work is most often found among the workers. If they do not participate in developing their own standardized work there is a risk that they will attempt to prove that the standard does not work in practice. Thus, when members of the workforce create their own standardized work there is a greater chance that it is accepted.

People outside the process also tend to describe the standardized work in more detail than necessary. The workers doing the work every day usually know better than others what is important to describe and what is obvious and thus unnecessary to describe. Obvious details should not be described in standardized work as it is then easier to quickly arrive at a suitable level of detail.

The presentation of the standardized work has much bearing on the degree it will actually be used to support daily work. Employees who are allowed to design their own standardized work will make it as simple as possible. Apart from the fact that simple standardized work is easy to adopt and use, it is normally also easy to update. In some types of operations it is difficult to make a stepwise description of the way of working. In these cases a checklist may be an alternative. An appropriate checklist is formulated so that the user has to take direct action, e.g. not only visually inspect that the tap is off but also manually check that it is so. This reduces the risk of overlooking any instruction in the checklist.

The content of standardized work will normally differ according to who created it. When members of the workforce are allowed to create their own standardized work they normally strive to design the work in such a way that the easiest way to perform a task is also the correct way of doing it. Equally simple solutions are not usually created by people outside the workforce. Forming the standardized work in a way that makes it easy to get it right improves the possibilities for it being adopted.

Giving the workforce the authority to create their own standardized work does not have to imply that management has little or no control of how the work is performed. After all, management has the overall responsibility for how the work is done. Normally, there is an overview within management and support functions that is required to judge how a change of the standardized work affects subsequent process steps or product quality. One way to deal with this is to let the members of the workforce propose their own standardized work and make sure that it is approved by management or a support function before it is applied.

The following steps can be distinguished in creating standardized work:

1. Train the organization to understand the need for standardized work
2. Create a first rough draft for standardized work
3. Test the standardized work
4. Define the duration of the standardized work

For standardized work to be successful, no matter how good it is, everyone involved must understand why standardization is important. Sometimes there is built-in resistance against standardization and this resistance can only be overcome through increased understanding.

The next step is to create a first rough draft of the standardized work for each work task. Making a note of part numbers and work sequences is a good start. Other important information that should be included is information related to e.g. safety and product quality. The required torque is an example of such important information. At this point, the standardized work is still at a rather rough level.

PART DEVELOPMENT	Process: Final assembly Part: Base coupling BK5 Department: Assembly Date: 2008-01-22	Sign:	Shift 1	Shift 2	Shift 3	Superv.	Engin.	Qual.

Standard Work Sheet

#	Work elements	Time: Man.	Auto	Walk	IMPORTANT! Safety, Quality, Engineering, Cost
1	Fetch base unit BE-996				
2	Connect base unit in fixture				
3	Fetch coupling KO-18				
4	Assemble coupling on base unit				
5	Fetch two pipes RR-89				
6	Place pipe and tighten				C Torque 15 Nm
7	Fetch hose SG-001				
8	Assemble hose on pipe				
9	Fix hose in fixture				
10	Start press				! Risk of pinning
11	Fetch housing HO-21				
12	Take finished part, connect housing				Q Visual control
13	Leave finished part				
	Total:				

! Safety | C Critical operation | Q Quality check | V Variant

Work sequence

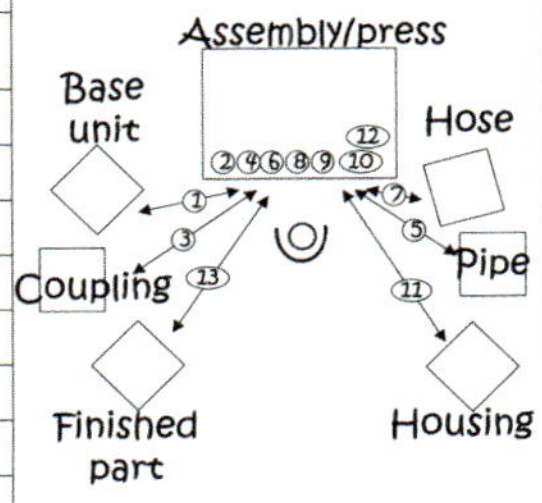

© Part Development AB

Figure 4-3. *Example of a simple standardized work.*

When the team has agreed upon the content of the standardized work for a certain work task, it is time to test it in daily work. By applying the standardized work over and over again, suggestions normally arise as to how it can be improved.

A standardized work that only states what should be done and how it is done is normally sufficient to achieve homogeneous product quality. However, in order to create conditions that improve the efficiency of the operations, it is also important to define the duration of the standardized work. This means defining an agreed duration of each work task during normal operating conditions. Measuring time can be as easy as using a stopwatch. A necessary prerequisite for defining this duration is that a common way of working is applied. Otherwise the defined duration has no value.

PART DEVELOPMENT	Process: Final assembly		Shift 1	Shift 2	Shift 3	Superv.	Engin.	Qual.
	Part: Base coupling BK5							
	Department: Assembly	Sign:						
	Date: 2008-01-22							

Standard Work Sheet

#	Work elements	Time Man.	Time Auto	Time Walk	IMPORTANT! Safety, Quality, Engineering, Cost
1	Fetch base unit BE-996			5	
2	Connect base unit in fixture	6			
3	Fetch coupling KO-18			6	
4	Assemble coupling on base unit	8			
5	Fetch two pipes RR-89			6	
6	Place pipe and tighten	12			C Torque 15 Nm
7	Fetch hose SG-001			5	
8	Assemble hose on pipe	5			
9	Fix hose in fixture	4			
10	Start press	2	5		! Risk of pinning
11	Fetch housing HO-21			6	
12	Take finished part, connect housing	14			Q Visual control
13	Leave finished part			8	
	Total:	51	5	36	

! Safety | C Critical operation | Q Quality check | V Variant

Work sequence

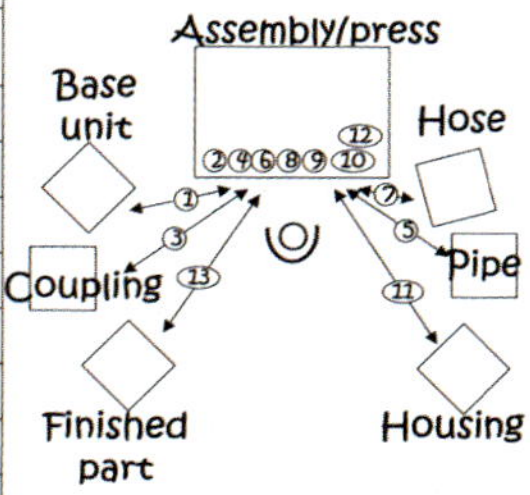

Figure 4-4. *A standardized work with a defined duration.*

A standardized work with a defined duration is also needed in e.g. the change-over of a machine from producing one part to producing another. When this kind of standardized work has no defined duration, it implies that as long as the end result is the same it is just as normal for the change-over to take four hours as one hour. This of course is not true. By following a certain work procedure as described by the standardized work there is also a defined duration of the change-over. Thus, with a standardized duration it is possible to detect deviations in allotted times. Resolving these deviations will in time lead to improved efficiency. Ways to resolve the deviations include more extensive training, purchase of new tools, etc. Continuous follow-up of deviations from the defined duration of an activity will eventually lead to more leveled and predictable operation times. Making a process more predictable is an important step towards making the whole flow more efficient.

Standardizing the duration of an activity is usually the most troublesome part of standardized work within non-manufacturing operations. A common problem within administration, services and healthcare is that there are a large number of products and product variants and that they are also difficult to identify.

However, having a large number of products does not mean that it is impossible to standardize the duration of the respective activities. It is rather a question of the level of detail. Most often it is possible to categorize the products in order to reduce complexity. Such categories are denoted product families, which will be treated in Chapter 6. Having well-defined product families, the standardized work for each category of products is ascribed an approximate duration. For example, quotations could be divided into small, medium and large, and a defined duration could be given for creating a quotation within each category.

As mentioned earlier, product development is a type of operation that entails a relatively large amount of creativity. It is commonly believed that the development of a new product cannot be ascribed a defined duration. However, breaking down product development work to the activity level normally shows that similar types of activities are repeated in every product development project. Certainly the size of the project may differ but the defined durations for activities can be adjusted correspondingly. The key to success in using defined duration in this kind of operations is to refrain from being too detailed and to make as accurate a judgment as possible so that there will actually be a defined duration to which the present value can be tuned. This entails that time will actually be discussed and deviations thus revealed.

An approximately defined duration is better than no defined duration at all. In addition, some kind of time estimate is necessary to determine capacity. How otherwise would it be possible to plan e.g. the manning of a service operation if there are no proper data on the time required to provide the service to the customers?

Documenting Standardized Work

The need to document a standard is dependent on what kind of standard is under consideration. In our private lives we may all have some standards that support us in our daily life. Some of us perhaps always put wallet, keys and cell phone in the hall just inside the outer door when we get home. In this way we do not have to spend time looking for them when we are in a hurry to get to work the next day. This is an example of a standard that concerns only one person and that has no related requirements concerning quality or duration time. It is hardly necessary to document this kind of standard.

Figure 4-5. *Example of a standard that contributes to making daily life easier.*

In other cases the design and documentation of the standard have significant impact on whether the standard will be applied or not. A thick book that contains "everything" will in the great majority of cases not be read. In addition, it will be difficult for someone in the workforce to detect changes to such an extensive standard.

An effective standardized work is graphical, brief and describes only what is most important. Using pictures to show how a part should be affixed to a fixture is often a better way of explaining than trying to describe it unambiguously in words. Good examples of simple visual assembly instructions are those that come with IKEA products.

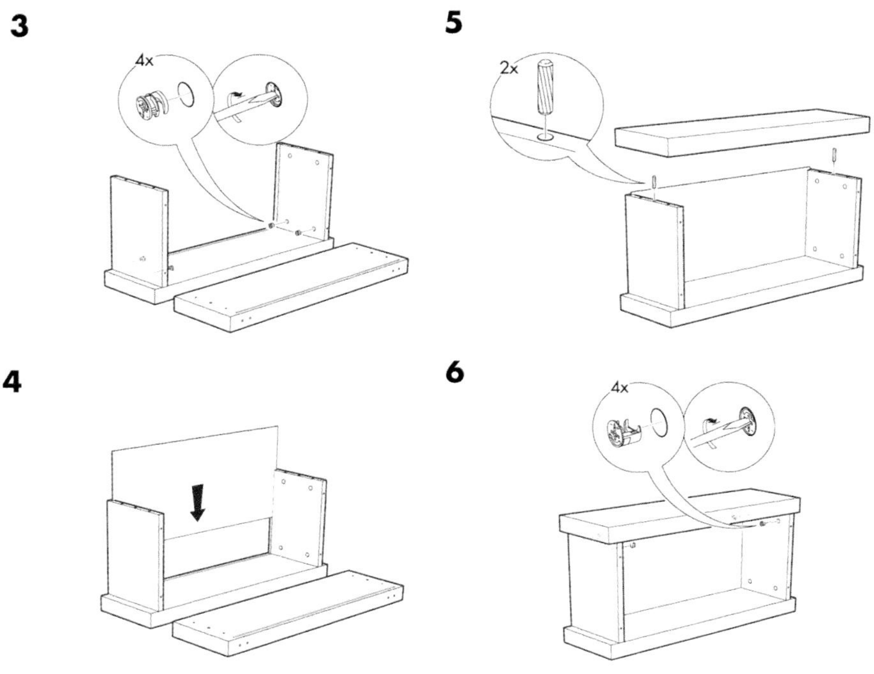

Figure 4-6. *Extract from an assembly instruction for IKEA MALM (© Inter IKEA Systems B.V.).*

It is important to point out that the example from IKEA has no defined duration, and assembly times will vary, since in this standardized work there are many opportunities to work in different ways at the level presented. Nonetheless, it is a good example of graphical illustration kept simple.

Following up Standardized Work

There is a close connection between standardized work and the Lean principle Takt. Applying standardized work is a condition for applying Takt to a process with high resource utilization. Applying Takt will in turn improve the possibilities to follow up if the standardized work is observed. In this way, the application of Takt is an aid in applying standardized work to daily operations.

From a theoretical point of view it is possible to apply Takt to a process without having standardized the way of working. However, to avoid continual stops this would require that the work content of each process step is significantly lower than the takt time. This means that only a minor part of the takt time is used for planned work. In this case it would probably be possible to maintain takt time even when the work is done in a less efficient manner than the best known. This is, of course, not desirable as it results in undesirably low resource utilization. There is also a risk that it will lead to low and unpredictable product quality that may be difficult to correct later on. Thus, to be able to successfully apply Takt it is important that the variations in time duration of each work task are as small as possible. This is also one of the main goals of standardized work.

In a process where Takt is not applied there is the possibility for the employees to work at the pace they desire. For some people this is a problem as their need to be on the safe side implies that they will always strive to produce too much rather than too little. The result is that they work faster than the demand rate, and working that fast involves a risk that shortcuts will be taken. A shortcut that would turn out to be illusory would be to deviate from the standardized work thus increasing the risk for injuries and decreased quality.

In a process where Takt is applied it would not be profitable to stress oneself or to take shortcuts that deviate from the standardized work. The product cannot advance faster in the flow solely because one person is ready ahead of time. In this way Takt is an aid in striving to standardize the way of working. Standardized work provides a solid foundation for efforts to achieve good ergonomics, high and consistent quality, and high productivity in manual processes.

Improving Standardized Work

Every improvement to an operation has a standard as its starting point, such as standardized work when it comes to ways of working. The standardized work improves as deviations are detected and solved.

Parallel to the introduction of standardized work it is important to perform in-depth training in the organization on the meaning of deviations, how deviations should be handled, and how the improvement work should be organized and structured. Solving deviations is the actual core of improvement work. Improvement work is treated in Chapter 5.

When a first rough draft of standardized work is adopted in the organization deviations will sooner or later appear. An assembly-related quality problem is one example of a deviation. Whenever there is a problem the following questions should be put *to the process* and not to the person:

- Has the work been standardized?
- Was the work performed according to the standard?

If the answer is that the work was not performed according to standard, the next step should of course be to extend training on why standardized work is important. If instead the answer is that the standardized work had been applied, it is a signal that it is not good enough, as deviations can still appear.

An overall illustration of improvement work is the so called Improvement wheel.

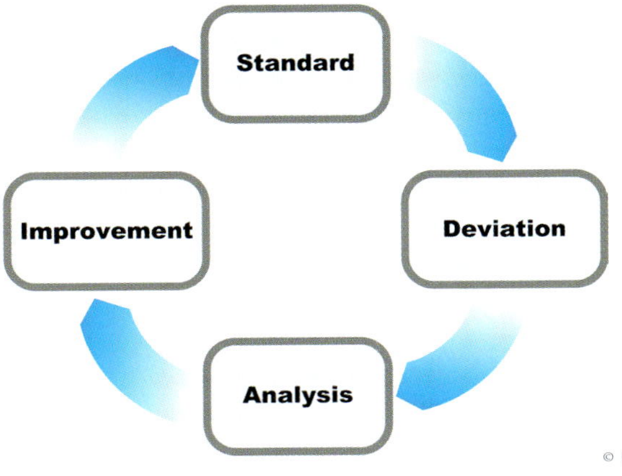

Figure 4-7. *The Improvement wheel.*

The Improvement wheel illustrates the improvement work outgoing from any standard or deviation. However, this section deals with improvements of standardized work.

The starting point is that a standardized work is required to detect deviations. A detected deviation has to be analyzed to enable choosing the right corrective measure. When the right measure is chosen the improvement can start. The improvement will not be completely finished until the standardized work has been updated. This because it is not until the standardized work is updated that there are proper conditions for the new and improved way of working to be applied.

There are some similarities between the Improvement wheel and the PDCA cycle. However, the Improvement wheel is more general in nature. PDCA is short for Plan, Do, Check, and Act and is a method used to structure improvement work. The PDCA cycle and its similarities to the Improvement wheel are described in the appendix.

As the standardized work is improved, the detected deviations will determine the level of detail. The standardization of a work task that has not had any deviations obviously does not need a higher level of detail. However, another standardized work may develop into a very detailed description because it has become obvious that this is needed. A detailed standardized work is normally not considered a problem by the workforce as long as the level of detail is based on actual deviations.

Standardization Forms the Foundation

Standardization forms the foundation for an organization's strive towards Lean. It is the basis from which all improvements are made and all improvements are formalized by updating the standard. From this discussion it follows that it is logical to complement the original Lean model by putting standardization in the foundation of the building. Standardization as such is a general term describing the best method, way of arranging tools, etc. that is currently known and agreed upon.

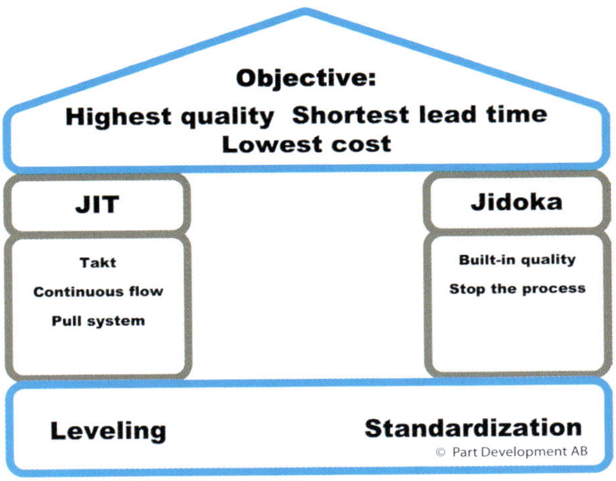

Figure 4-8. *Standardization is a part of the foundation of an organization's strive towards Lean. Therefore it is logical to symbolize standardization by placing it in the foundation of the Lean model.*

Standardization contributes to increased predictability in time as well as in quality. Thus, standardization supports both of the two main principles within Lean: JIT and Jidoka.

See the whole, but make improvements on the details.

5. Impro

Improvement Work – The Key to Success

For a Lean effort to be successful in the long term, a well established improvement program is required in which the entire workforce participates. If this is not in place there is a risk that the positive effects achieved in the short term will disappear, and the organization will revert to square one. In addition, it is often difficult to relaunch the Lean effort when it has previously failed.

Strive for Perfection

Improvement work aims at eliminating:

- Unevenness (Mura)
- Overburden (Muri)
- Waste (Muda)

Unevenness is the origin of other waste and it can be reduced by leveling workload in different ways. Leveling was described in Chapter 3. Unevenness also implies reduced predictability, which is a problem as predictability is an important basic component of an efficient operation.

Overburden means that resources are loaded to a level exceeding capacity. This can be avoided through leveling but also through improved balancing, i.e. a better way to distribute workload between resources. Balancing is further described in Chapter 6.

Waste is a central term within Lean. It means activities and occurrences that do not add customer value. This is the focus of daily improvement work at the workforce level.

Improvement work is so central in Lean that it is part of the visual Lean model. The roof of the Lean model symbolizes the ambition to achieve perfection, i.e. an operation that is free of unevenness, overburden and waste. The ambition is formulated as a vague world-class goal that encompasses highest quality, shortest lead time, and lowest cost. By striving for perfection the organization is encouraged to continuously question and improve its operations.

Continuous improvement is so fundamental to Lean that it is sometimes considered a main principle. However, every improvement springs from one of the two main principles JIT and Jidoka. Thus, continuous improvements entail applying JIT and Jidoka at new and higher levels, over and over again. This is the meaning of the expression to *strive* for Lean. An operation is Lean when it no longer contains any waste, but this is an unattainable state. Instead one is (or should be) always working *towards* Lean and thus continuously moving in the right direction.

Improvement work within Lean means eliminating waste from an operation in small and controlled steps. In this way the value-adding portion of the total activity increases, and this in turn means that improvement work is beneficial for the customers, for the workforce, for the owners as well as for society in general. For the customers and owners waste implies costs that they cannot accept. Society is favored by reduced waste because as organizations get more efficient they become more competitive. The more competitive organizations are, the better chances there are to maintain or even increase local employment. The workforce is negatively impacted by waste every day: by being irritated over malfunctioning equipment, overstraining legs by walking long distances, idling during waiting time, having to put in much overtime, etc.

It may be difficult to find waste to eliminate even when actively looking for it, and so everyone needs to be trained to detect waste. Basically, every activity can be divided into two parts:

- Value-adding
- Non value-adding (waste)

So far so good, but the question is how to make the workforce capable of detecting waste in the operations they have been working in for a long time. It does not take long before one becomes blind to the waste in one's work.

Seven Forms of Waste

For an operation to achieve excellent efficiency it is necessary that it is designed in such a way that waste may easily be detected. If this is the case there exist opportunities to eliminate, or at least reduce, waste. Designing an operation so that waste is exposed is sometimes thought of as making the operation fragile and, to a certain extent, vulnerable. This may be controversial as no operation is able to deliver on schedule if disturbances are too extensive.

However, by challenging the operation in a controlled manner it is possible to regulate to what extent deviations will be detected. This is often described by the well-known Japanese lake example. A controlled lowering of the water level in the Japanese lake, i.e. a controlled challenge of the operation, means that the reefs surface at a rate that the organization is able to handle. Improvement work means taking care of these deviations and making sure that they will never recur. And then a real improvement will have been made.

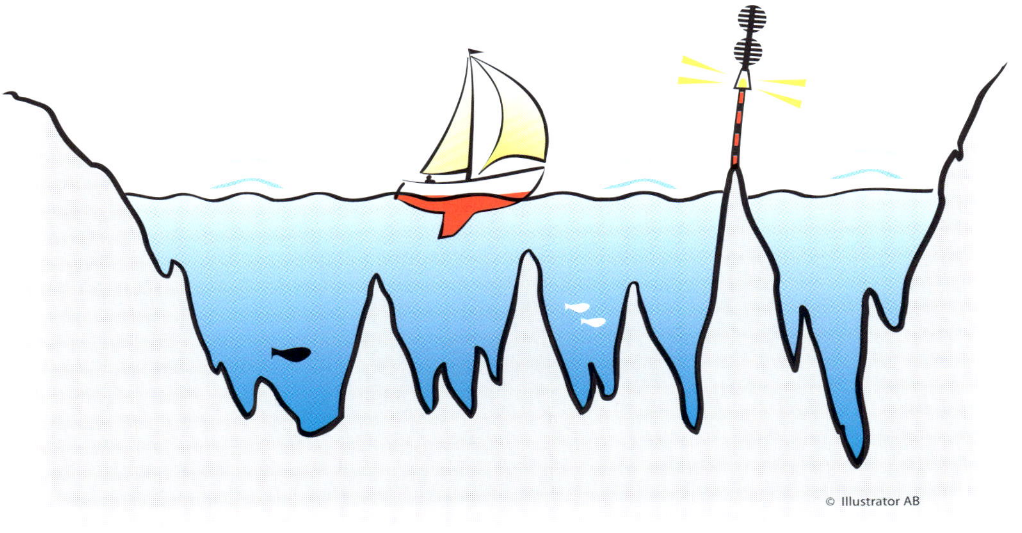

Figure 5-1. *The Japanese lake.*

An organization's ability to distinguish between the value-adding and the waste is a necessary condition for all improvement work. It is therefore important to raise the workforce's consciousness of improvement. Every employee should focus on reducing, and at best eliminating, all that is not value-adding. Seven forms of waste, and sometimes an extra eighth, are distinguished within Lean:

1. Overproduction
2. Waiting
3. Transport
4. Inappropriate processing
5. Inventory
6. Motion
7. Producing defective products
8. Untapped competence

Having these categories of waste as a starting point will make detection of waste easier. *It is looking at the operation from another perspective.*

Overproduction

Overproduction is usually considered to be the worst form of waste as it contributes to other forms of waste. Overproducing means producing more than the customer wants, producing faster or earlier than what is required by the next process, and producing overlarge batches.

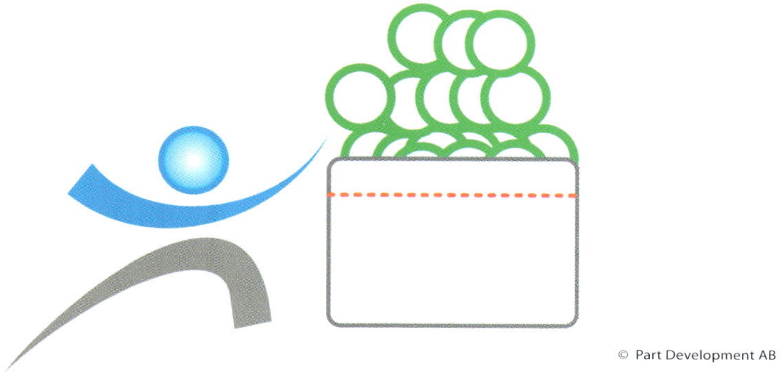

Figure 5-2. *Overproduction.*

Companies that solely produce to customer order may still be overproducing. For example, producing a customer order of 1000 units at the beginning of the month is considered overproduction if they are not to be delivered until the end of the month. What happens if the customer makes a late change to the order? Moreover, producing too early creates an unnecessary need for storage space.

A corresponding line of reasoning in healthcare is when patients waiting for surgery are admitted into the hospital although there is no time for surgery until much later. In administrative operations overproduction may be about entering or refining information that no one will use.

Waiting

This form of waste means time not used in production that is spent waiting for the necessary conditions. It may be due to a lack of material or a lack of information about what should be produced next. Waiting is a common form of waste in all kinds of operations. Waiting for people who are late for a meeting is a form of waste that, apart from the frustration it causes, leads to lost work time which in turn costs a lot of money.

Figure 5-3. *Waiting.*

The most striking example of waiting in healthcare is the patient waiting in various queues. Healthcare personnel also wait for other personnel, e.g. cleaning staff or a surgeon who will perform the surgery. In administrative operations waiting for information and decisions is common.

Transport

Transports add no value. The only transport that the customer is normally prepared to pay for is when the product is delivered to the customer. Internal transports, on the other hand, are pure waste. An important question is why there is a need for transports. The need for transports is a symptom of something else being wrong, e.g. the layout of the facility.

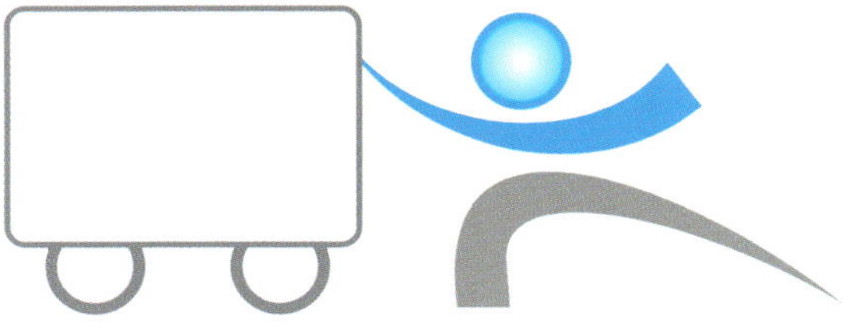

Figure 5-4. *Transport.*

Using forklift trucks (manual as well as automatic), conveyor belts, etc. is not a rationalization of transport but only a rationalization of the actual transportation work. This confusion often leads to focus being put on finding smarter ways to transport rather than on ways to eliminate the need for transports. It cannot be claimed that waste has been reduced until the need for transport has been reduced. Transport waste can be visualized by a Spaghetti chart, which is more closely described in the appendix.

Transport of test samples is common in healthcare. Sometimes the transport distance is great as a result of a functional organization with centralized resources.

Physical transports are not very common in administrative operations, but transportation of information is. Another example is log-ons and log-outs from various information systems. To visualize this kind of waste there are specific Spaghetti charts for information flows (see the appendix).

Inappropriate Processing

Inappropriate processing means performing more work than the customer is prepared to pay for. It may be producing to a higher quality than the customer is willing to pay for, or carrying out unnecessary tasks.

Delivering a product of too high quality will probably make the customer happy and impressed at the outset. However, after a while the customer will realize that this additional work also adds costs. Similarly, the customer does not want to pay for the execution of unnecessary tasks. An example of an unnecessary task is when too large blanks are used in the turning of parts. Much of the machining is done just to reduce the size of the blank to the correct dimensions. Purchasing a smaller blank would have avoided this unnecessary task and at the same time the smaller blank would probably have been less expensive.

Figure 5-5. *Inappropriate processing.*

Other examples of unnecessary tasks are tests and inspections. These kinds of activities are often considered necessary, but are in fact waste. The underlying reason for this waste is unreliable processes. Thus, it is important to find the root cause by asking *why* the tests and inspections are needed. In healthcare, taking several identical test samples from a patient can be viewed as inappropriate processing.

Parallel documentation is another example of inappropriate processing which occurs in most activities. It means that a number of people document the same thing. Apart from being wasteful it may cause problems if the parallel versions do not conform. Another example is when a number of people spend time reading a patient's journal prior to surgery instead of having a common verbal briefing of the relevant information.

Inventory

Large storage spaces, buffers and inventories are often a necessity because the delivery processes (internal or external) cannot always deliver as promised. Another reason for the need to store may be that the purchasing department received a large discount when ordering the whole year's consumption at once. This kind of "savings" may be expensive in terms of total cost as it ties up capital, requires storage space, hides problems, etc. Another drawback of inventories is that they prolong lead times, which in turn reduces the ability to rapidly adapt to changes in customer demand. In addition, large inventories entail a larger risk when e.g. quality problems are uncovered, if the customer makes changes, or even goes bankrupt.

Figure 5-6. *Inventory.*

Low interest rates are a common argument to justify large inventories. The reasoning behind this view is that it is less expensive to be "on the safe side". While it is true that inventories are less expensive when the interest rate is low, would it not be better if the tied-up capital was used in profitable investments? In addition, there is also the risk of the inventory becoming unsalable.

Motion

Motions that do not add value are obviously waste. This could entail e.g. walking to fetch tools and materials. Another example is when the tools are placed in such a way that the operator has to bend or stretch to reach them. Apart from the fact that these motions are unnecessary, they may also be harmful from an ergonomic point of view. Non-value-adding motions and poor ergonomics obviously also exist in healthcare and administration, e.g. lifting heavy objects, straining in awkward positions, searching for people, or equipment placed impractically with long walking distances as a result.

A good work environment is of utmost importance to the employee as well as to the company/organization. An occupational injury is not only a personal catastrophe for the employee but also a failure for the organization. There are many good reasons to put effort into creating a good work environment. It is important for the organization to have a good reputation which will attract the best workforce. In addition, in many countries the financial consequences for the organization are severe when employees incur work-related injuries.

There is also a large potential for improving productivity when the operations are designed in such a way that unnecessary motions are eliminated or at least reduced. How much would productivity increase if the workforce enjoyed the right working conditions, as for example to be positioned in the right way with the right tools in the right places?

Figure 5-7. *Motion.*

Producing Defective Products

Producing defective products gives rise to waste since what was not done right from the start has to be corrected. In many cases entire expert departments are established to deal with this kind of waste. Not many customers are willing to pay for that.

A common example of defective products is input data incorrectly filled in, e.g. incomplete order information or incorrectly filled in referral forms. Other examples from healthcare are inadequate treatment and hygiene that lead to patients getting healthcare related infections needing treatment.

Instead, the resources should be spent on finding the root causes of the defects. Where are the defects produced and what are the reasons why things were not done correctly from the start?

Figure 5-8. *Producing defective products.*

Untapped Competence

This form of waste is actually an addition to the seven forms of waste described above. By missing the opportunity to use the competence of every member of the workforce, there is a risk of losing employees as well as missing the improvements that the organization would have been able to implement.

An effective way of increasing the use of the competence residing in the workforce is to integrate the work content vertically: aim for competence in depth in a narrower field over broad but shallow competence. Competence is not better utilized by fastening screws at several different assembly stations, but by working at a single assembly station and thus having the possibility of becoming highly proficient at that task. In this way the worker develops a sense of ownership and responsibility towards that work station and will strive to improve it by eliminating waste. This supports the individual's personal development at the same time as the employer benefits from always accessing more of the workers' growing competence.

Figure 5-9. *Untapped competence.*

Untapped competence, or unused creativity as some prefer to call it, is the most common label for the eighth waste. It should be mentioned that some organizations choose other meanings for the eighth form of waste than the one described here. This may be because they want to focus on an area that they find extra important. One such example is safety; in this case the aim is to emphasize that both incidents and accidents are forms of waste.

Other Forms of Waste

The categorization into seven plus one forms of waste is common within manufacturing. However, as described above, these forms of waste can be found also in non-manufacturing operations. Nevertheless, there are other ways of categorizing and naming waste. Examples of other forms of waste that are mentioned in the literature are:

- Efficient production of the wrong product
- Untapped human capital
- Inappropriate systems
- Waste of energy and water
- Waste of natural resources

One example of waste categorization, intended for service companies, views waste from a customer perspective:

- Delay
- Duplication
- Unnecessary movement
- Unclear communication
- Incorrect inventory
- Opportunity lost
- Errors in the service transaction

Yet another categorization lists the following 14 forms of waste:

- Sorting and searching
- Inappropriate measurement
- Underload
- Overload
- Inappropriate prioritizing
- Interference
- Inappropriate frequency
- Start up and end off
- Mistakes, errors or lack of appropriate knowledge
- Misunderstanding or communication errors
- Sub-optimization
- Waiting
- Inappropriate presence
- Inappropriate tradeoff

It is in fact not important for the improvement work how waste is titled or how it is categorized. The categorizations and names are there to make it easier for us to understand what waste actually is, making it easier to detect waste. The categorizations are rough and they do not give information on exactly what has to be done to reduce, or at best eliminate, waste. In order to be able to get down to the level of detail required to actually perform an improvement the operation must have the ability to detect deviations.

Distinguish between Product and Process

All improvement work in all kinds of operations should question and develop the *process*. Working with the process is also the way to improve the *product*.

The process is *how* things are done, the product always being a result of the process. Making this distinction is normally not a problem in the manufacture of physical products, but it may be more difficult in non-manufacturing operations.

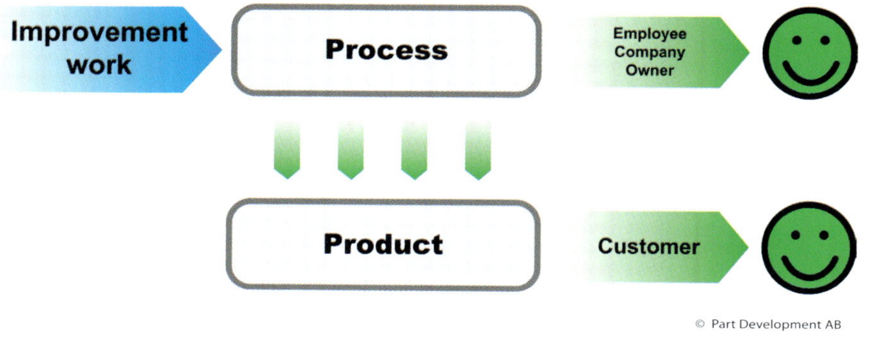

Figure 5-10. *All improvement work is about improving the process, also in those cases where it is the product that is considered to be the problem.*

Deviations may be related to the product as well as to the process, but the cause of the deviation will always be found in the process. Thus, a product-related deviation such as a quality problem can have its cause in either the product development process or in the manufacturing process.

The cause of a product design problem should be sought in the product development process in the same way as the cause of a manufacturing-related problem should be sought in the manufacturing process. When the cause is identified, the necessary corrective actions can be taken.

> *"It is not the product itself but rather the process of producing the product that brings long-term success. Good products do not create winners. Instead, winners produce good products."*
>
> (Translated from Sandkull and Johansson, 2000)

Different Forms of Improvement Work

Kaizen is a Japanese word that is also commonly used outside Japan. Kaizen stands for continuous improvements and its approximate translation is "change for the better". Standardization is a necessary prerequisite for Kaizen, as all improvements have to start from an agreed understanding on how things should work.

Most organizations claim that they work with continuous improvements. But often their improvement work is limited to documenting the things that need to be improved. If there is no structured procedure, it will be difficult to realize an idea and to implement the improvement: one will not progress beyond the written document. In order to achieve real results, there must be no uncertainty as to what should be done, who will be responsible and when it should be finished.

Continuous improvements are applicable to anything. In the manufacturing industry, Process Kaizen and Flow Kaizen are common terms. Process Kaizen aims to improve a specific process while Flow Kaizen aims to improve the flow that links processes together. Both forms of Kaizen are important, but as the flow affects the conditions for, as well as the requirements on, the individual processes it is often more effective to start out from the flow and let the desired flow put requirements on what improvements need to be done at the process level.

In addition to Kaizen, i.e. continuous improvements of the daily operations, there are two other forms of improvement work:

- Kaizen Event
- Kaikaku

Kaizen Event is a form of improvement work where different stakeholders gather for one or more days to solve a specific problem or a specific kind of problem. An example of a kind of problem that may be suitable for a Kaizen Event is to find the causes of, and solutions to, a specific type of quality problem. A Kaizen Event can be viewed as an intensive workshop performed at Genba. At a Kaizen Event a workshop leader is chosen who is responsible for leading the workshop and following up on results.

Kaikaku means "radical change" and it is a form of improvement work that is carried out as a project with well defined and quantified targets. A Kaikaku involves not only parts of the manufacturing staff, but also resources from e.g. product design and manufacture supporting functions. It is not unusual that a Kaikaku goes on for up to one year and sometimes even longer. An example of an improvement assignment that is normally performed in the form of a Kaikaku is creating an entirely new production set-up. The targets of such a Kaikaku may be improved production control in order to achieve shorter lead times, reduction of tied-up capital and improved delivery reliability.

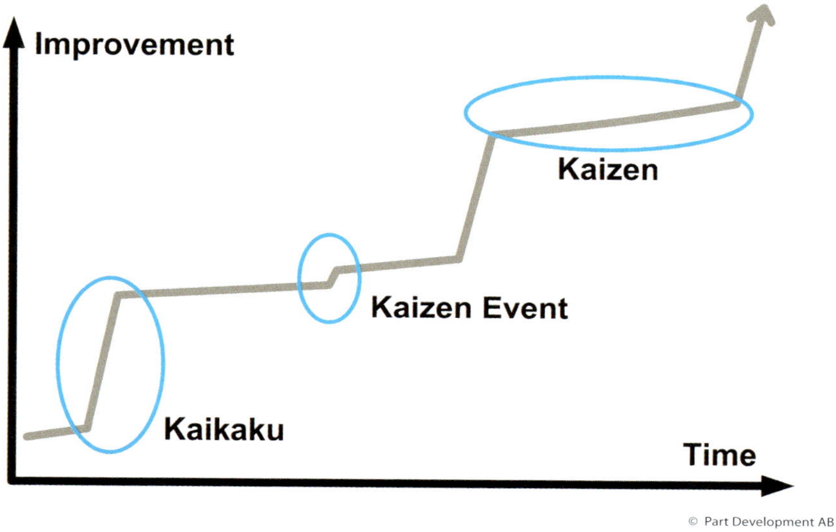

Figure 5-11. *The different forms of improvement work have different temporal characteristics and different functions along the way towards an improved operation.*

Kaizen Events and Kaikaku are often effective ways of solving larger and more complicated problems. However, unlike Kaizen these two forms of improvement work are tied to specific points in time. This raises the risk that the workforce will wait for these occasions, thus delaying improvements. Kaizen Events and Kaikaku should be viewed as complements to Kaizen, i.e. to the continuous improvement work that should be a natural part of daily operations.

Kaizen may be the most important element of an organization's Lean effort. The physical restructuring of flows and the application of new methods are important ingredients in an organization's Lean effort. However, without an effective improvement work it will be difficult to take advantage of the improved conditions given by e.g. a new layout, introduction of Takt, etc. The main distinguishing feature of companies that have been successful in adopting Lean as a way of relating to their operations, is that they have managed to develop a self-sustaining improvement work effort in which as many members of the workforce as possible are involved and committed (at best, all of them...).

Working with Kaizen is working with the small details: the problem as well as the solution lies in the details. Dealing with a problem at an overall level is impossible when you want to succeed with an improvement. To put a point to it, it can be stated that it is impossible to improve product quality at the overall or macro level. However, it is possible to introduce guiding sticks to the assembly of gaskets on a certain product variant. This will in turn improve quality.

In all improvement work it is important to see the whole while simultaneously making improvements on the details, otherwise there is a risk that when a detail is improved it will not impart any improvement to the whole. Why prioritize reducing cycle time by one minute in an automatic process when the equipment has excess capacity at the current demand rate? Had the equipment been a bottleneck in the flow then the priority would have been more than justified. A holistic view provides a certain natural order of priority.

Deviations – The Fuel of the Improvement Work

Standardization is the starting point of the improvement work as it is a prerequisite for being able to detect deviations. When it is not possible to tell what is normal it is impossible to tell what is abnormal. The abnormal, i.e. the deviations, constitute the necessary fuel for an effective and enduring improvement work effort.

If improvement work is solely based on turning good ideas into practice it will soon fade out. After a while the energy to come up with new ideas will disappear, and the result is artificial improvement work where improvements are made without considering the whole context.

As we have seen, eliminating all waste from an operation is impossible. There will always be deviations in all processes, no matter how good those processes become. Toyota has been working with continuous improvements since the 1950's and they still have deviations in their operations. However, as the operations are improved, the deviations normally get smaller and more specific. In a situation where the deviations are considered to be too few it is time to challenge the operations in some way so that new deviations appear. In this way new fuel is added to the improvement work, and the improvement work will continue and never come to an end. In order to get a quick opinion on the maturity of the improvement work it is good to ask members of the workforce what is their *smallest* improvement. When the answer is a very small process-related improvement this indicates that there is a good understanding of what continuous improvements actually mean.

The more detailed the standard, the smaller deviations can be detected. In spite of this, many organizations restrict their work to the really large deviations. The reason is that the deviations are sorted in pareto order and from that list the largest ones are chosen as they have the largest impact on the result.

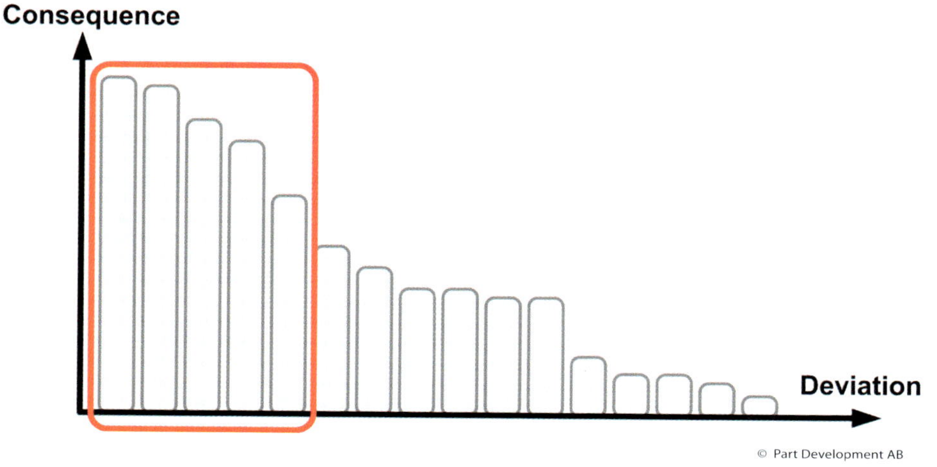

Figure 5-12. *Pareto chart where the five deviations with the greatest consequences are marked.*

Deviations that have major consequences can either be individual major deviations, or a number of smaller repeatedly occurring deviations. Working with only the individual major deviations carries the risk that the improvement work will fade out. This because large deviations normally take a long time to solve and they also often require specialist knowledge. To make improvement work exciting it is important that the employees get the opportunity to "win victories" as often as possible, even though the victories may be small.

Minor deviations have the advantage that they are normally easier to solve than the major ones. In addition, the fact is that the large problems that an organization is facing often started out as minor disturbances. Thus, it may be effective to treat them as early as possible before they grow into major problems. On the other hand, the major deviations normally have severe consequences which means that they cannot be ignored. Therefore, in order to achieve an effective improvement work it is advantageous to work with a mix of major and minor deviations.

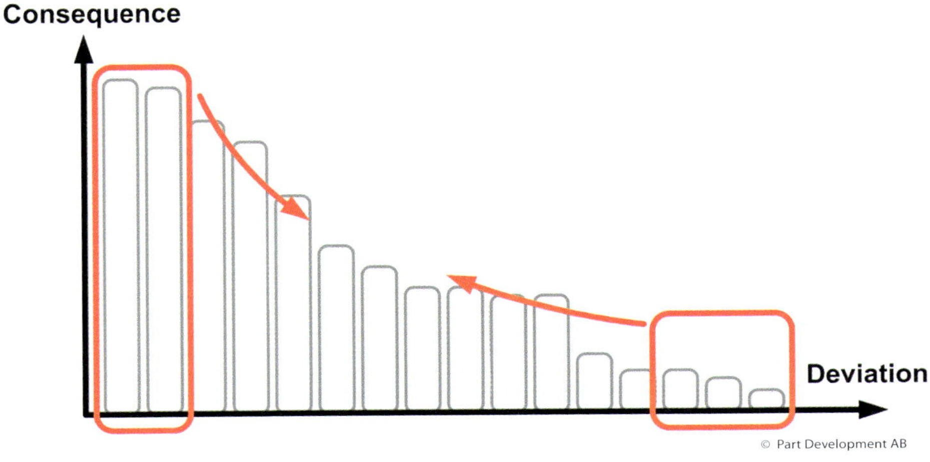

Figure 5-13. *Effective improvement work deals with a mix of major and minor deviations.*

The Workforce Drives the Improvement Work

In an operation that has come far on its journey towards Lean, the members of the workforce own their processes and are responsible for developing their part of the value stream. To make it possible for the employees to take on this responsibility, it is important that there is an organizational structure to support them.

The road towards an effective improvement work effort starts with the conviction that the team is stronger than the sum of its individuals. It may therefore be wise to organize the workforce into some kind of improvement teams, where every team is responsible for e.g. a physical area, or a part of a value stream.

The responsibility and the authority that come with process ownership entail that everyone in an operation striving for Lean has two equally important parallel tasks:

- To produce (products, care, services, etc.)
- To improve the operations

Figure 5-14. *The improvement team members drive the improvement work together.*

In certain ways, members of the workforce take on the role of process engineer and problem solver. This is a role that has traditionally belonged to various support functions.

Problems are solved and ongoing improvement issues are followed up within the improvement team. However, in some cases it will be impossible for the improvement team to have the time to handle all the deviations that have been detected. Some problems may also require additional investments or specialist knowledge that the improvement team may lack. In cases like these managers as well as support functions are important resources for the improvement team. Still, it is important that the responsibility for solving the deviations stays with the improvement team. The improvement team drives and follows up the work of solving deviations also when the actual problem solving is performed somewhere else in the organization. The manager's role in this context is to encourage and support the improvement team instead of controlling problem solving in detail.

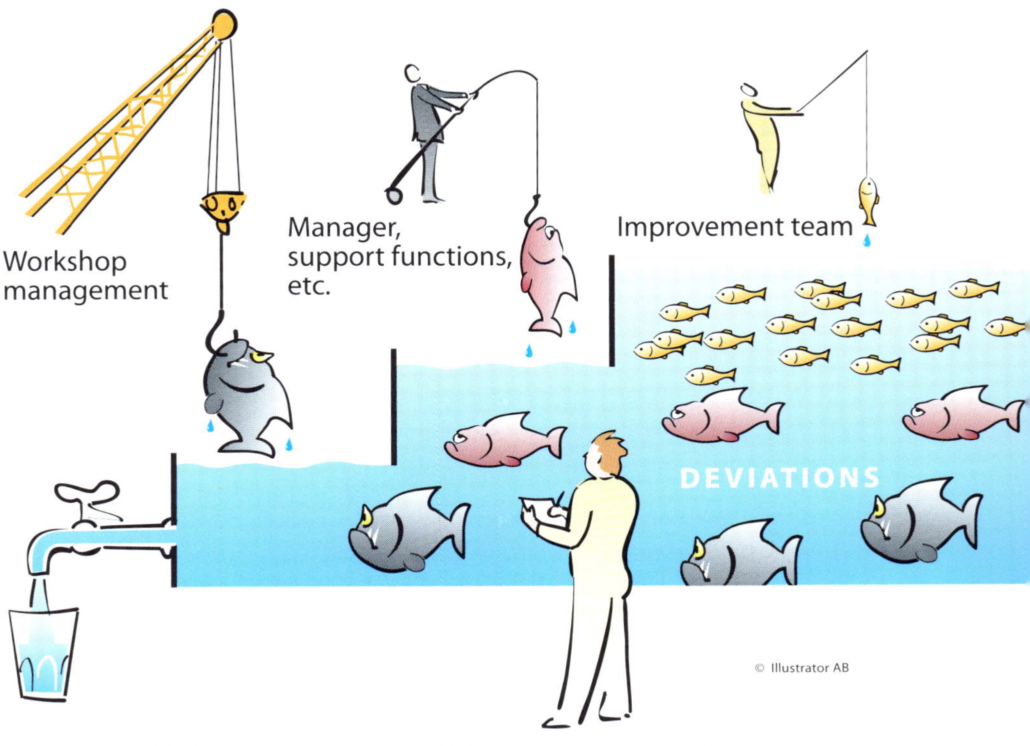

Figure 5-15. *The improvement team owns ALL deviations but it may need support.*

The efforts of the whole workforce to improve operations together are crucial for the organization's long-term ability to be successful with its Lean effort. To underscore this fact, it is logical to place the decisive role of the workforce at the centre of the visual Lean model. Every person's contribution to the team is what gives life to the Lean effort in real life. It manifests itself in the form of waste reduction through a continuous search for new and better ways to apply the Lean principles.

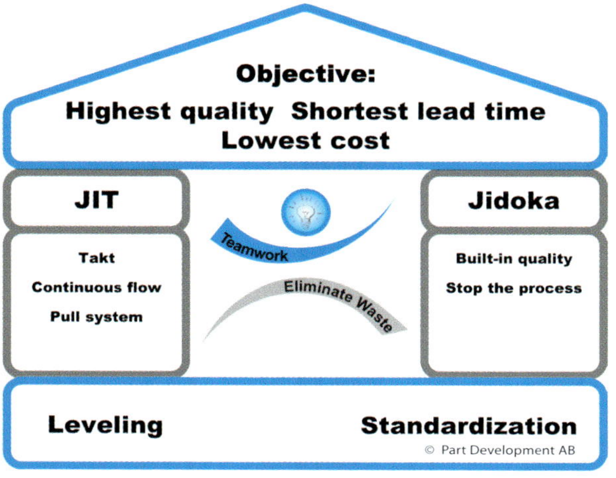

Figure 5-16. *The human being at the centre of the Lean model as a symbol of the work-force's crucial importance for a successful Lean effort.*

The Board – The Hub of the Improvement Work

For the improvement work to be effective, the deviations detected need to be structured in some way as it is normally impossible to deal with all the deviations at the rate they appear. A simple board located where the operations are performed may be a good way to present the deviations as well as the ongoing work of solving them.

A notice board of the type shown in Figure 5-17 is an effective tool for displaying information on the deviations that are being worked on at the moment, who is responsible for each deviation, and when each improvement task should be finished. The members of the workforce can also use the board to continuously make notes of new deviations that have been detected in the operation. In this way, all information will be found at one spot and be available to everyone at the workplace (at Genba).

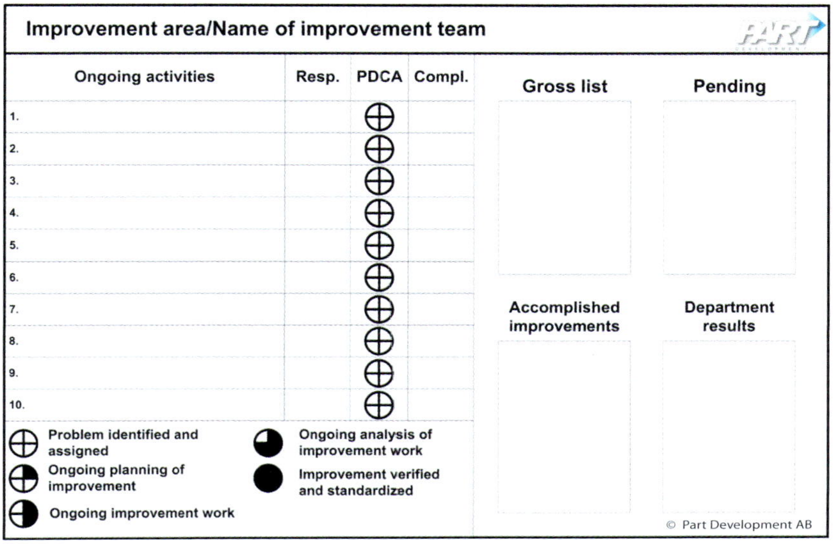

Figure 5-17. *Example of improvement board design.*

The improvement board constitutes a natural hub for team members to meet around for joint meetings on a regular basis. At these meetings the aim is to follow up the status of ongoing improvement tasks, and to make decisions on how new deviations should be prioritized and assigned to the team members. It is not a meeting for problem solving because in order to make the improvement work efficient the actual problem solving should be done between meetings.

Work as presented on the improvement board should be a consequence of detected deviations and not only a collection of good ideas. This in turn requires that the operation is challenged at a level where deviations can be detected. When the improvement work is based on actual deviations, the risk of wasting improvement resources on issues that will not improve the operation is minor.

In a flow where Takt and standardized work are applied, the members of the workforce will continuously detect deviations. The deviations are noted on a "Gross list" on the improvement board. The Gross list is a list of all deviations that have been detected but not yet dealt with. Thus, it is a kind of waiting list.

When a deviation is detected it should also be analyzed. Analyzing a deviation means identifying the actual reason why it occurred, the root cause. When the root cause is found, a solution can be chosen which will ensure that this specific deviation will never recur. This is an important step for the improvement work to be successful. However, it should be mentioned that it may be difficult in real life to have time to instantly analyze every deviation. In these cases the operation should instead focus on collecting as many facts as possible about what happened, so that the deviation can be analyzed at a later stage.

The analysis method 5 Why, which is described in the appendix, is often suitable for finding the root cause of a deviation. The example in Figure 5-18 shows how deviations detected when applying Takt can result in concrete improvement measures.

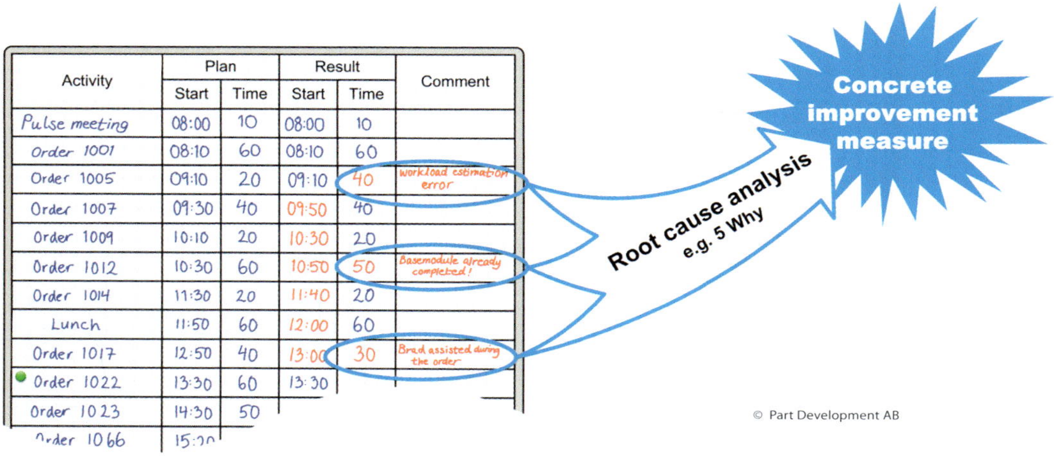

Figure 5-18. *Example of how the application of Takt can result in concrete improvement measures.*

In this example the application of Takt has resulted in the detection of three deviations. A brief comment describing each deviation in more detail serves as a basis for analyzing the deviation using e.g. 5 Why. Note, in this example two of the deviations consist of used time being shorter than planned time. Considering this as a deviation entails possibilities to determine whether e.g. quality was jeopardized, or whether there was a lesson to be learned about how the activity could be carried out more efficiently. When the deviations on the Gross list exceed what the workforce can handle before the next improvement meeting, the deviations have to be somehow prioritized. As previously mentioned it is preferable to have a mix of large and small deviations in order to keep up the pace of the improvement work while major consequences due to large deviations are reduced. The large deviations are normally those where the improvement team needs support, from e.g. a support function. The members of the team take care of the smaller and more manageable deviations by themselves. In prioritizing between deviations a PICK chart may be helpful. The PICK chart model was originally developed by Lockheed Martin and PICK is an abbreviation of Possible, Implement, Challenge and Kill. In a PICK chart each deviation is assessed based on what the effect would be if the deviation is solved and on the effort required to solve it.

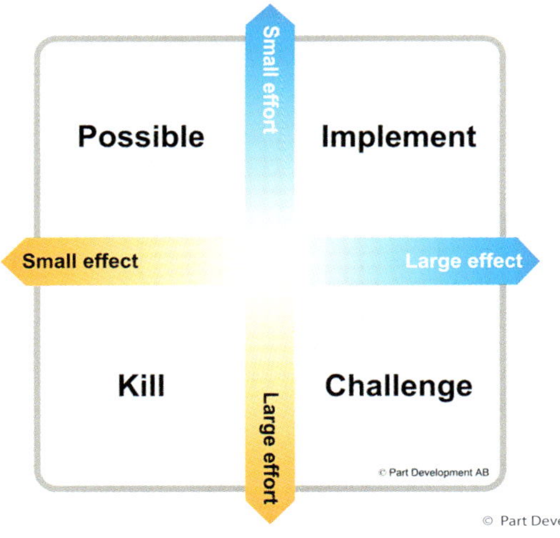

Figure 5-19. *PICK chart for prioritizing deviations.*

An advantage of the PICK chart model is that it provides structured support to the members of the workforce in their deliberations concerning appropriate priorities. A deviation resulting in extensive consequences but only requiring a small effort to solve ends up in the field *Implement* and will thus be given high priority. On the other hand, if a deviation ends up in the field *Kill* it will be quite easy to decide not to deal with it as it will simply not be profitable. Deviations that end up in the field *Challenge* require larger efforts to solve. Thus, these are the kind of deviations where the improvement team may have to call for support from the rest of the organization to find a suitable solution and put it into practice. Deviations that end up in the field *Possible* have lower priority than those in the field *Implement*. It means that these deviations will be dealt with only when the improvement team has time to do so.

New deviations are moved to "Ongoing activities" when there is an empty row. A row in Ongoing activities becomes empty when an improvement task has been carried out. A simple PDCA circle may be used to continuously visualize the progress of a certain improvement task. The PDCA cycle is described in the appendix.

An implemented improvement task is moved to the so called "Accomplished improvements" list, which is a list of the improvements made by the improvement team. The Accomplished improvements list is not an absolutely necessary item on the improvement board but it may contribute to motivating the members of the improvement team. As improvement work is preferably carried out in small and controlled steps it is easy for the members of the workforce to feel that nothing is happening. Therefore, by periodically checking the Accomplished improvements list it will be obvious to everyone that the improvement work actually brings results. In addition, the Accomplished improvements list can easily be referred back to if a deviation, contrary to expectations, were to recur. In that case the Accomplished improvements list will show when measures were taken, what they were and who took them.

Some deviations are such that the improvement team is normally unable to solve them on their own. These may be deviations that also affect other departments, that require decisions on investments, or require specialist knowledge. Even these kinds of deviations should have an appointed responsible person in the improvement team. This person is responsible for the activity and the deviation should be entered on the "Pending" list. In this way the activity is visualized as ongoing despite the fact that no one in the improvement team is actively dealing with it. To be successful, this way of working requires that the section receiving a deviation also prioritizes solving it. If the answer times back to the improvement team are normally too long there is a risk that improvement team motivation will diminish.

Leadership in the Improvement Work

Working with continuous improvements in the way described in this chapter requires a great deal from management. It requires leadership that in many aspects is different from the leadership models that have prevailed through the years. In the distant past the manager was almighty and everyone was expected to do as he or she ordered. Later, at the end of the 20th century, autonomous groups were in focus which resulted in a leadership that more or less abdicated. In some cases the teams of employees could do what they wanted as long as they achieved the desired results. Under this kind of leadership, the teams had much influence but they lacked support on how to do things. It would be interesting to see a high-jump coach saying: "Jump any way you like as long as you clear 2,40 meters".

Figure 5-20. *A high-jump coach who is not interested in jump technique will probably not be successful with his novice.*

The leadership required to be successful with continuous improvements (Kaizen) is situational, supportive and at hand. The workforce must feel that they can, and moreover are expected to, influence their own situation. The manager should support the teams. In the beginning the support is to a large extent confined to encouraging and leading the team forward. With a more mature improvement organization, the supportive role is more about e.g. pleading the improvement team's cause with other departments. Other examples are putting demands on internal customers and suppliers and confronting upper management in investment matters.

A successful leader in an organization that has come far on its journey towards Lean is interested in the details of the operations. Of course, he or she does not need to know all the details, but it must be understood that the details are important. The sum of all details builds the whole and all real changes have to be made at the detail level.

The leader's authority is to a large extent based on his or her understanding of the Lean principles and the operations at hand. By leading the way with practical examples at the workplace, the leader shows that the right results will come when the organization consistently applies agreed ways of working.

The leader's way of behaving in various situations is of crucial importance. The signals sent out by the leader have a major impact on the organization's ability to detect the deviations that actually constitute the organization's potential for improvement. If the management in words and behavior shows that the detection of deviations is a necessary condition for improvement, they will shape the organization into a deviation seeking force. The opposite case, where management sees deviations as obstacles preventing the organization from reaching its goals, results in the workforce turning a blind eye to waste.

When the organization realizes that detecting deviations is something positive, improvement work has come far. No one will hide problems in such an organization, instead those who expose problems will get credit. Thus, the organization needs to start liking deviations!

Figure 5-21. *The goal is to make the organization like deviations.*

The improvement work has an aim and a meaning: To improve the value stream.

6. The V

The Value Stream – The Improvement Arena

> *"Whenever there is a product for a customer, there is a value stream. The challenge lies in seeing it."*
>
> (Rother and Shook, 1998)

All improvement work takes place somewhere in the value stream. It may be in individual processes or in connections between them. In the end, the improvement work aims to improve the value stream as a *whole*. However, creating smooth and predictable processes is necessary in order to provide the necessary conditions for developing efficient and predictable value streams. It is in the flow that the various processes become linked together into a totality. It is this totality that affects the ability to deliver the right product at the right time and at a low cost.

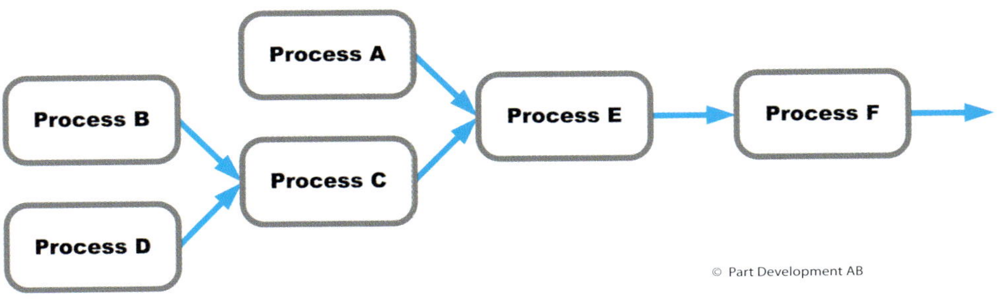

Figure 6-1. *The value stream is made up of connected processes.*

In addition to the product's flow through the processes, the value stream also comprises the flow of materials to the processes, and the flow of information needed for the value stream to function and to produce the right product at the right time.

Analyze the Value Stream

An operation's success is heavily dependent on effective improvement work in the entire organization. It is important to differentiate improvements from changes. A change in operations does not necessarily mean that something is affected for the better, only that it has been changed. The improvement work has an aim and a meaning and when it comes to Lean that aim is improving the value stream. A thorough analysis of the value stream reveals what activities are necessary to actually improve the value stream. In this way the risk of choosing sub-optimizing activities is reduced.

As a parallel to how value streams should be analyzed, it may be interesting to look at how a physician should act when examining a patient. The patient arrives, feeling pain somewhere and describes the symptoms to the physician. The physician asks questions and performs tests to get a full picture of the patient's state of health. Problem causes are excluded one-by-one and the root cause is found. In this way a correct and effective method of treatment can be applied instead of some general treatment that may not bring the desired effect. What is the reason why the patient has a headache? Without a thorough analysis, totally irrelevant measures may be recommended. Has the patient hit her head? Is it related to stress or are we dealing with more complicated diseases like cancer? Thus, a casual prescription of two aspirins is too general a treatment method.

Figure 6-2.

Without a thorough analysis of the problem there is a great danger that incorrect measures are taken.

To be meaningful, all improvement work should have a problem or a business opportunity as a starting point. The problems and opportunities referred to here are always somewhere in the value stream and the challenge is to find the cause-and-effect relationships.

Start from the Customer Values

The analysis of a value stream should start from what adds value to the customer, as this indicates what the customer is willing to pay for. Without this knowledge, it is difficult to say exactly what is value-adding and what is waste. When the communication between customer and supplier is limited to the contacts taken between buyers and salesmen, there is a risk that parts of the customer's actual requirements and desires are overlooked. Some examples of questions that may be relevant in this context are:

- Is the product produced and packed in such a way that it does not imply unnecessary handling in the customer process?
- What are the requirements and the desires of those receiving the product at the customer site?
- What end-customer requirements may have been ignored by the first customer in the supply chain?

Customer requirements are more than just price, quality and delivery reliability. In order to improve the flow correctly it is necessary to know what really adds value to the customer. What is it in each work task that the customer is willing to pay for? A rough rule of thumb is that activities that in some way change the product add value while other activities are waste. This is true within manufacturing as well as within other types of operations. The value-adding portion of the total work is normally considerably smaller than the portion that is waste. Within manufacturing, the value-adding time is often measured in minutes while the total lead time is measured in weeks or months. Also in administration, services, healthcare, etc. the value-adding time is only a small portion of the total lead time.

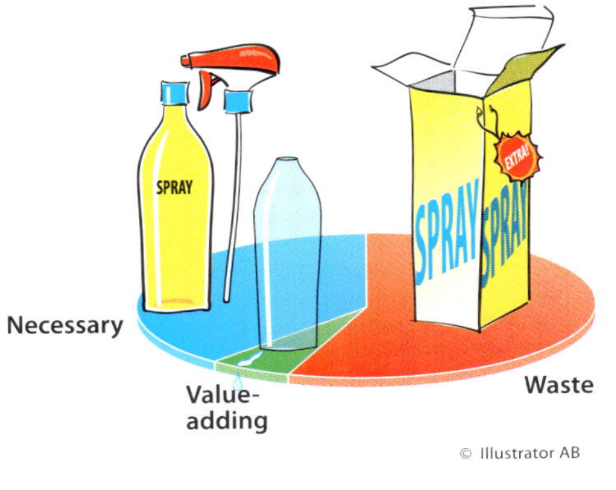

Figure 6-3. *Common proportions of value-adding time, time for necessary but non-value-adding activities, and time spent on waste activities.*

In addition to value-adding activities and waste, necessary but non-value-adding activities are normally recognized. These are activities that under given circumstances are necessary to perform and therefore cannot simply be eliminated. Examples of such activities are cleaning of equipment, packaging of products in protective packages, and transports to the customer. In some cases the terms value-adding and waste are interpreted in a very strict manner, and then *all* activities can be categorized as either value-adding or waste.

Create Product Families

Most operations produce many different products. In many cases it would hardly be possible to analyze every product separately and then create a unique flow for each product. In any case such an exercise would take a long time. In order to avoid work being halted because it is too complex to analyze all products, it may be efficient to work with product families.

A product family is a grouping of products that does not consider attributes like appearance, customers or volume. Instead, a product family is distinguished by the fact that the products pass through the same processes, preferably in the same sequence. In order to be able to divide the products into product families, their value streams must be analyzed. The compilation of the results of the analysis is preferably done in a product/process matrix.

Product/Process Matrix © Part Development AB

Product number	Press 1	Press 2	CNC 2	CNC 3	Weld 1	Weld man	Blast	Paint	Pack	QC
700294-2	X		X			X	X	X	X	X
234422-2	X		X			X	X	X	X	X
300245-1	X		X			X	X	X	X	X
893874-1			X		X		X	X	X	X
373733-0		X		X	X				X	
806058-4		X		X	X				X	
8466599		X		X	X				X	
8467663		X		X	X				X	
2664883	X	X			X				X	X
101010-2	X	X			X					X
277347-9		X	X				X	X	X	
998345-7		X	X				X	X	X	
720806-1	X			X	X	X	X	X	X	X

Figure 6-4. *Example of a product/process matrix with three different product families marked.*

When the product families have been identified, their respective value streams can be analyzed separately. In this way the work effort required is reduced as the number of product families is generally considerably less than the number of products.

Product Families ***Example***

In healthcare there are many different care chains that run partly in parallel, but come together at various centralized functions. A care chain can be viewed as a product family which could perhaps be entitled patient family. The advantage of categorizing into patient families is that complexity can be reduced. Patients with similar complaints basically follow the same care chain even though they are not treated in exactly the same way. The differences may for example depend on the severity of the complaint or on the overall health status of the patient.

The fact that patients within the same patient family basically follow the same flow makes it possible to create an effective flow for a certain, relatively known volume of patients. Treatment of e.g. a typical uncomplicated fracture normally follows a certain plan. The radiotherapy department is a common example of a function where many care chains meet. To minimize the negative effects on each care chain/patient family it is required that there is a clear set of rules at such meeting points.

Collect Data about the Flow

Accurate knowledge of the current situation is essential for ensuring that a change will be an actual improvement. It is not enough to know *approximately* how things work and *approximately* how the customers behave. All relevant facts have to be mapped and this mapping makes it possible to determine the flow's conditions and characteristics in detail. Examples of relevant data are:

- Frequency of delivery
- Variations in customer demand
- Flow paths
- Actual capacity
- Batch sizes
- Production control

Value Stream Mapping is a relatively simple and common method to explore a flow and to collect the necessary data about the processes in question. The method Value Stream Mapping is described in the appendix.

The frequency of deliveries from the value stream affects the possibilities of controlling production. It is important to know *when* the deliveries take place. If deliveries take place once a week, once a day or every hour makes a big difference.

Frequency of Delivery *Example*

In administrative departments data are sometimes registered into information systems that will not pass on the information until later, e.g. every night. Therefore, in this case the frequency of delivery is once per 24 hours. In healthcare the frequency of delivery may be how often patients are released from a nursing ward. Is it once a day, or does it take place continuously?

It is also important to know the day-to-day variation in total demand rate. Knowing that the customers order 5000 units of a certain product per year tells us nothing about the capacity that is required in the short term. If there is a big variation in daily demand rate, then either capacity or the finished goods inventory must be adapted to this. So, the average demand rate does not provide sufficient information on what is needed in terms of capacity or buffers.

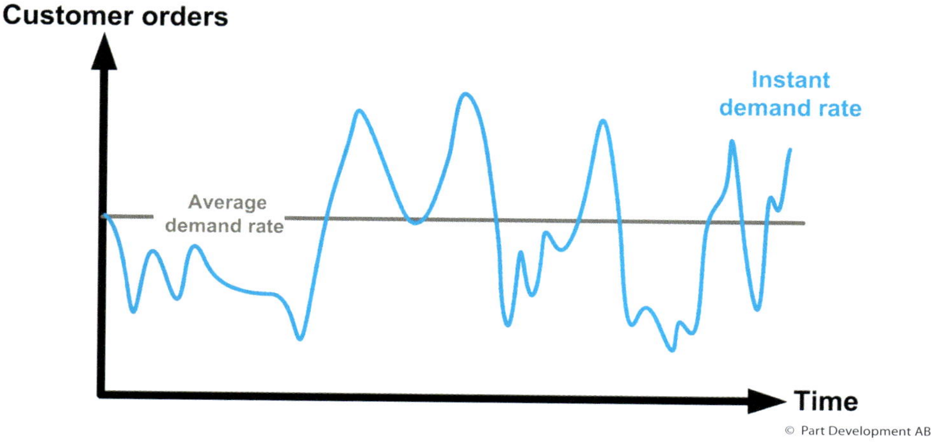

Figure 6-5. *Example of variations in customer demand rate. High sampling rates enable accurate detection of variations.*

Information on averages is not particularly useful in the analysis of a value stream as it generally does not correspond to the actual real life situation. For example, families with 1.66 children are quite rare.

Exactly what the demand variations will look like in the future is, of course, impossible to predict. However, by analyzing historic data it is normally possible to get a relatively good indication of the characteristics of the variations that can be expected.

Variations in Customer Demand ***Example***

The perceived variations in customer demand are affected by how each member of the workforce plans his or her work. If someone chooses to collect all referrals in a pile before they are reviewed and passed on to the next authority, the receiving department (secretary and time booking) will experience larger variations in demand than if the referrals were to arrive one at a time.

Other important data that must be collected are how products, materials and information move along the value stream. This is knowledge that many people claim to possess even before the mapping has started. However, all too often these opinions of how things are thought to be do not match the actual conditions. There may be several reasons why the flow has changed over time, two common examples being that new and undefined intermediate inventories have been introduced, or that unofficial production control methods have been initiated to parallel the official ones.

Flow Paths ***Example***

One example of a flow path is an administrative product's way through the value stream. The flow path can be described by mapping where value is added to the product and where it waits to be refined. It is not unusual that for the same kind of administrative product there are a number of alternative and dissimilar flow paths.

Analyzing flow capacity is a central part of data collection. In order to gauge the value stream's ability to respond to customer needs it is the actual capacity of each process that is of interest. Actual capacity is the capacity that a process can attain in reality. This means that in determining actual capacity, the expected or known deviations in the form of quality losses, stops, etc. must be considered. So we see that determining the actual capacity requires detailed knowledge about these types of deviations in each process.

Actual Capacity ***Example***

Actual capacity can be expressed as the number of surgical operations performed per time unit, the number of orders registered per time unit, or the number of served customers per time unit. A requirement for being able to determine the actual capacity is that there is standardized work, and that every work standard has a defined duration so that there are representative time data available. It is also necessary that there is knowledge about how closely the standard times are maintained on average, as well as knowledge about quality yield.

Collecting data about batch sizes is important as these affect the flow capacity as well as the flow's ability to respond to customer demand within agreed time frames. Large batch sizes imply that the number of change-overs can be reduced, and this means that a larger amount of the planned production time can be used for production. One reason for having large batch sizes, but strangely enough not the only one, is long change-over times. The change-over time is the time it takes to switch over a process from producing one product to producing a different one. In some cases the change-over time is considered a fixed parameter that has to be accepted. This is not true however, as it is always possible, to some extent at least, to reduce change-over time.

Batch Sizes *Example*

Batch size refers to how much work outcome is kept together before being delivered to the next step in the value stream. It may concern a process that stores basic purchasing data for many different parts, and passes them on as one batch. In this case the batch size is equal to the amount of basic purchase data being sent. Another example is an electronic mailbox that is emptied only once a week. In this case the batch size cannot be expressed in number of emails, as it is impossible to know how many emails will be received during the week. Thus, in this case batch size must be expressed in terms of time, i.e. the batch size in this example is one week´s worth of emails.

It is not unusual that a flow is deemed to lack capacity although it can be shown by capacity analysis that it actually has excess capacity. One reason may be that the way the process is planned and controlled implies that the process is being loaded with the wrong products at the wrong times. This, in turn, implies that the products demanded by the customers may not be finished in time. Too large batch sizes may be the reason for this. However, if the capacity analysis shows that there is excess capacity, then the possibility to reduce batch sizes exists, while at the same time the ability to produce sufficient volumes per time unit will be preserved. Using excess capacity to perform change-overs will cost little or nothing when the resources are available and have already been paid for. The advantage of reducing batch sizes is that the flow is improved resulting in improved delivery reliability and lower total cost.

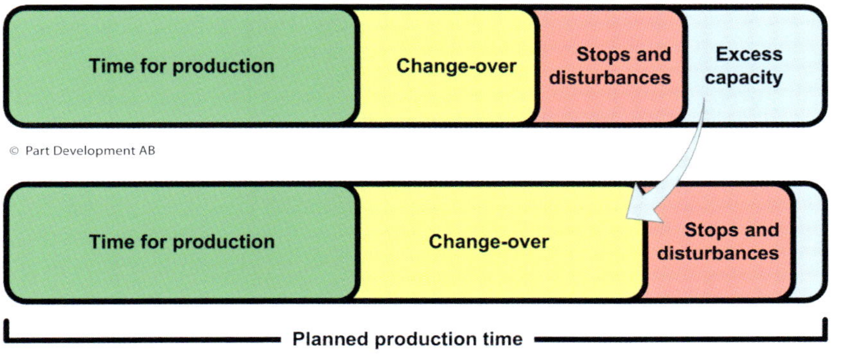

Figure 6-6. *Using excess capacity to increase the frequency of change-overs will result in an improved flow at little or no extra cost.*

Production Control ***Example***

Production control concerns what should be done and when, as well as how the person executing the task receives the signal that something should be done. In some administrative processes the employees receive a list of what should be done during the coming week. In this case, production control is nothing more than this list. The list does not specify more than that certain tasks should be executed some time during the week. Thus, there is great freedom of personal choice, but it is at the cost of low predictability of task completion time. The problem with this situation is that it will be difficult to plan the entire flow of administrative products. At the same time it will be difficult to track the operation's progress.

Design of the Value Stream

The design of the value stream determines how efficient a flow can be. A proper flow design creates opportunities for the products to pass through the flow as fast as possible, and in the desired order (sequence). The flow should moreover be designed in such a way that deviations are easily detected. Revealing deviations is important in order to be able to improve the value stream.

The opposite of revealing flows are robust flows. Robust flows are flows that can handle most problems that may arise in a flow, minor deviations as well as major ones. For a manager under pressure it may, of course, be comforting to know that the safety net is so extensive that not even large deviations in the operations will affect deliveries. However, the disadvantage of robust flows is that they hide deviations. In fact, some smaller deviations may never be detected. Larger deviations will probably be detected anyway but it is normally difficult to find their root causes. Thus, the main disadvantage of robust flows is that they hide deviations and do not provide the right opportunities for improving the flows. All the hidden waste in a robust flow costs large amounts of money and these are naturally costs that the customer is not willing to pay for.

Thus, one should always aim to design revealing flows in which deviations are detected easily and rapidly. Detecting waste is necessary to be able to reduce, and at best eliminate, waste. However, the step from a robust flow to a more sensitive one is daunting and there should be a preparedness and the means to handle temporary production backlogs in the flow. Perhaps the way to proceed is adding production time or having a relatively large finished goods inventory so that the flow can deliver, at least in the short term, if the problems become too extensive. As deviations are resolved and the flow becomes more stable, this capability to handle production backlogs can gradually be reduced.

In principle, a production flow consists of three parts:

- Product flow
- Material flow
- Information flow

The product flow refers to the product's path through the value stream, while the material flow describes the supply of material to the product flow. The information flow describes the flow of information that controls production as well as material supply.

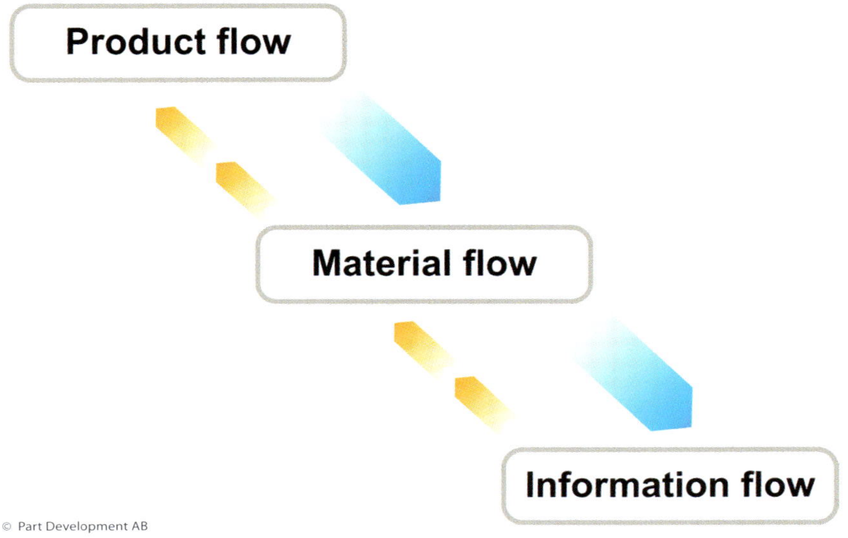

Figure 6-7. *Desired sequence in designing the three parts of the production flow. To some extent the design process is inherently iterative.*

Design of Product Flow

The product flow is the part of the production flow that should be developed first. It has the highest priority as this is where the refinements that generate revenue are made. The product's path through the value stream should be flow-oriented in order to create the best conditions for Takt, Continuous flow and Pull system. In addition, simple and direct flows should be chosen instead of parallel or partially parallel flows. Partially parallel flow means that the flow diverges and/or converges, and this is likely to entail control problems.

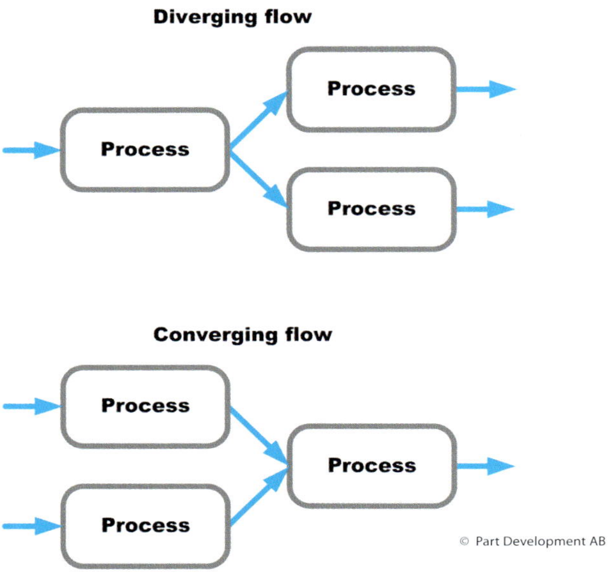

Figure 6-8. *Diverging and converging flows respectively.*

An important reason to strive for simple and direct flows is to reduce the number of planning points in the flow. A planning point is a point in the flow where decisions are made on what should be produced next, i.e. the possibility to make a choice. However, where there is a possibility to choose there is also a risk of making the wrong choice. Naturally, this problem can be reduced by instructions and rules, but to completely eliminate the possibility of choosing is a better solution as it improves the chances of getting it right from the start. In a direct flow there is only one planning point and that is at the beginning of the first process. This being the case the subsequent processes have only to continue refining the products that arrive and to do so in the same order (sequence) as the products arrive.

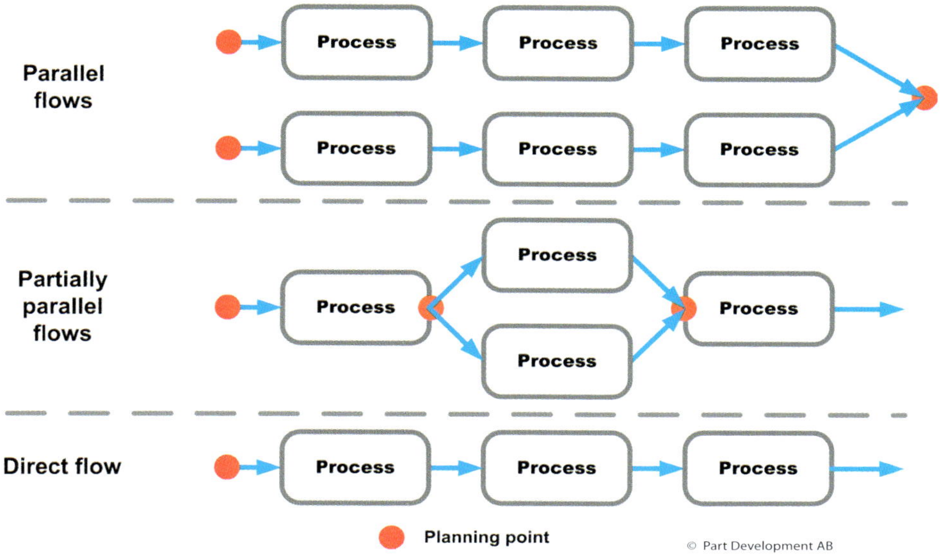

Figure 6-9. *A direct flow has the least number of planning points. It brings the most predictable result in terms of maintaining a given sequence throughout the product flow.*

When a buffer between two processes is introduced, an additional planning point is introduced as well. This means that also a direct flow has more than one planning point when there is a buffer between two processes.

The number of planning points has a major impact on the ability to maintain a given production sequence through the whole flow. If the flow starts with a leveled production sequence, the ability to keep this order through the flow is important. If the sequence changes, the positive effects of a leveled flow are lost. A small number of planning points, moreover, makes it easier to keep to FIFO (First In, First Out) throughout the flow. This is important for quality reasons.

The design of a product flow should also provide the right conditions for applying Takt to the flow. Here too direct and simple flows are preferred. With *one* direct flow the entire production activity has one common and clear takt. A single direct flow also entails shorter takt time since the entire volume is produced in one flow. This is important in cases where the takt time is considered too long to support an efficient application of Takt. When the takt time is too long it is more difficult to detect waste. In contrast, shorter takt times make it easier to detect even the smallest deviations as production is followed up more frequently.

Product Flow *Example*

The patients' path through the care chain may, by definition, be viewed as an example of a product flow. Another example is the flow a referral passes through from issuer to recipient. A product does not have to be physical but can just as well take the form of compiled data in some electronic format. A product flow within non-manufacturing operations typically consists of value-adding processes, non-value-adding processes, and intermediate storages (buffers) of e.g. information.

Non-manufacturing flows have planning points in the same way as do manufacturing flows. For example, administrative flows are often less controlled than are manufacturing flows, which implies that they may have considerably more planning points. Two examples of planning points in an order flow are: the members of the workforce can choose themselves in which sequence the received orders should be processed, and there is a freedom of choice regarding to which person the order will be passed for further refinement.

Design of Material Flow

The material flow, similarly to the product flow, should be designed based on the Lean principles. In addition, it should be adapted to the conditions given by the product flow. Flow design is to some extent an iterative process where repeated fine-tuning of the product flow design may be required in order to achieve a satisfactory material flow.

Similar to the design of the product flow, the material flow should be designed in such a way that direct and simple flows are achieved at the same time as unnecessary movements are avoided. Short transport distances and material close to the point of consumption should be in focus. These desirable attributes are also valid for internal supplies such as preassemblies, which should be placed as close to the customer process as possible, not only to achieve short transport distances, but also to strengthen the customer-supplier relationship.

Intersecting material and product flows should be avoided as far as possible, as they may otherwise disrupt each other. Re-picking material is not value-adding and should therefore be avoided whenever feasible. Instead, actions should be taken to improve the presentation of material in a way that supports the user. In addition, small package units are advantageous in the entire supply chain.

In order to minimize buffer levels and to avoid unnecessary material handling, there should be just one point of consumption for each part. Another important aspect of material flow design concerns the localization and dimensioning of buffers. In general terms, buffers should be as small as the prevailing conditions allow. The buffers should be placed where they are needed from a value stream point of view and not where there happens to be available space.

Design of Information Flow

The last piece in the production flow design puzzle is the information flow. The information flow should support the product flow as well as the material flow. When designing the information flow it may be necessary to make changes to the product flow and/or the material flow in order to secure a good result at the holistic level.

The Lean principles, together with simplicity, should be in focus in the design of the information flow. Most crucial is to find a simple way to transfer the demand signal between the processes, i.e. to apply the Pull system. Further, it is important to create conditions that permit the use of as up-to-date information as possible, since this will make the flow less sensitive to e.g. late changes in customer orders. The information flow should also be designed in such a way that it will be easy for everyone involved to understand the information correctly, i.e. it should be easy to get it right.

Standardization of the Value Stream

The term standardization is relevant not only to processes but also to value streams. Standardization of the value stream can be viewed as a description of, and an agreement on, how the flow should work. Actual capacity is naturally of great importance to the flow and the factors that affect actual capacity should therefore be standardized. Batch size is an example of such a factor.

All improvement work is aimed at improving standards, and it is equally important to improve flow related standards as to improve process related standards. However, in order to achieve a good practical solution that will be designated a standard at the flow level, it is required that the standards at the process level are sufficiently good. This, as every process should produce predictable results in terms of quality and time.

Standardization of a value stream means defining and agreeing on how the flow should work. All the factors of the flow that affect performance need to be defined. Examples of such factors are:

- Flow design
- Products/variants
- Variations in demand per product and variant
- Actual capacity
- Batch sizes
- Location and size of buffers
- Planning
- Control

Standardizing a flow creates important conditions for detecting what is abnormal in the flow. The detected deviations constitute a source of improvement that will never dry up, and, if dealt with properly, these deviations can take the business to superior levels.

Flow Preparation

The agreement on how the flow should work can be likened to the basic production data that are the result of production preparation. Production preparation starts from design data usually consisting of one or more drawings. The design data is then translated into production data that comprises a practical solution on how to produce the product at the right quality and with the desired efficiency. However, sometimes it is necessary to redesign the product. The final basic production data resulting from the production preparation process is a work instruction. This work instruction constitutes an agreement between the designers and the production personnel on how the product should be produced.

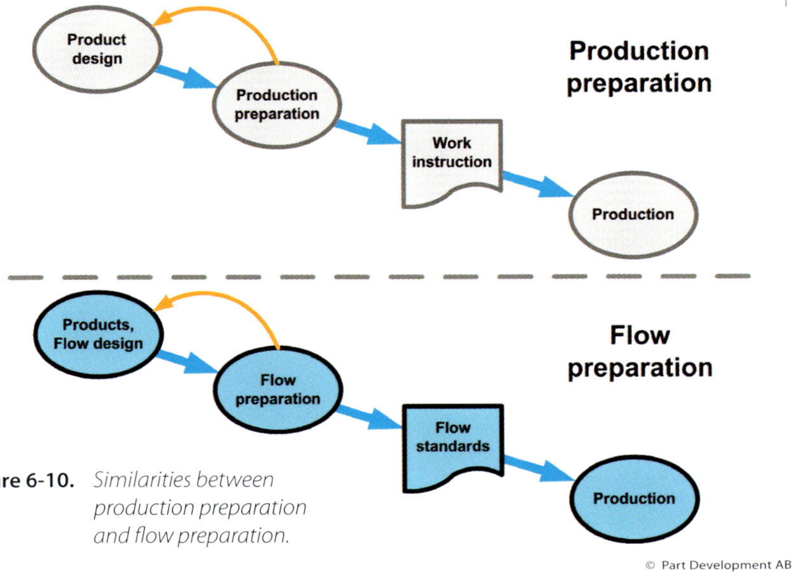

Figure 6-10. *Similarities between production preparation and flow preparation.*

The production flow needs to be prepared in the same way, so that an agreement between the concerned parties on how the flow should work is created. The process of creating standards for the flow is in this context referred to as flow preparation. The starting point for flow preparation is the flow design and the products that are to be produced in the flow. Given these, the flow is then prepared in detail. It sometimes happens that flow design has to be changed, or that some products need to be transferred to other flows in order to achieve a flow that is sufficiently efficient. Flow preparation entails that all the parameters and activities affecting flow performance are analyzed and defined. The result is a description of how the flow should be designed, dimensioned and controlled. When an agreement is reached that these descriptions are valid, they are promoted to standards.

Flow Preparation ***Example***

In non-manufacturing operations flow preparation concerns designing, for every product family such as patient- or service family, the various parts of the flow and agreeing upon how they should interact. The goal is to achieve the best possible quality and service for the customer, at the same time as costs are kept low. When solutions are found, they should be standardized and followed up as part of the daily operations. Applying standardized work to the interactions between flow parts is a means of detecting deviations. Solving these deviations will improve the flow step by step.

Connections between Processes

To make a production flow predictable, well-defined rules on how the flow should work are required. Given that there are defined standards in the respective processes, the next step is creating standards for the connections that link the processes together.

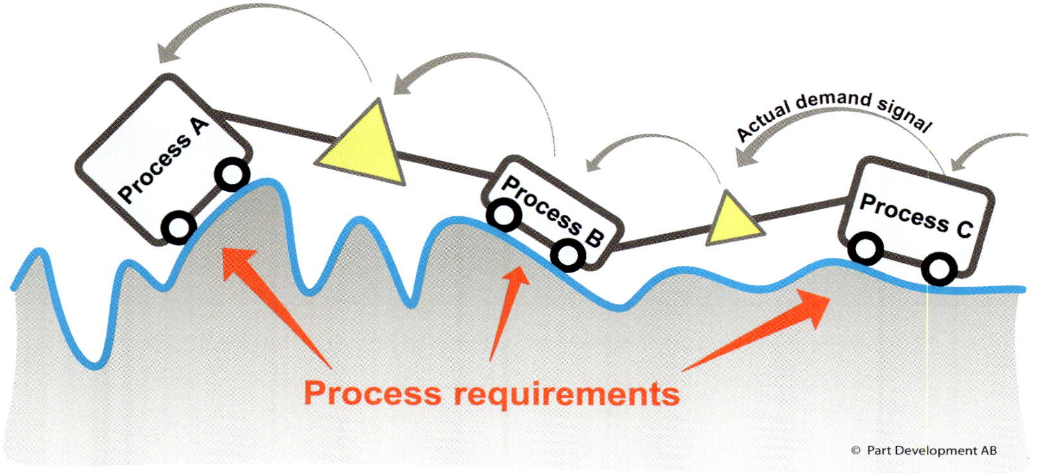

Figure 6-11. *In analogy to the wagons of a train, there are connections between the processes of a flow.*

To achieve efficient flows, well-defined connections between the processes are necessary. These must be updated as conditions change over time: there may be changes in takt or the product mix, variations in customer demand rate, etc.

The connection between two processes is primarily made up of agreed rules on how the two processes should work together. One aspect that is necessary to define is how the customer process is allowed to request products and materials from the supplying process. There should moreover be rules on what actual capacity each process should have, as a balance in capacity between the processes is desired.

In addition to balanced capacity, it is also desirable to have simultaneous capacity. This means that both processes should have the same work hours so that they produce simultaneously. When this is not the case then there is a need for an additional buffer. This leads to an unwanted disconnection of the processes, which in turn makes it more difficult to transfer the demand signal from the customer process to the supplying process sufficiently fast and with unchanged content. When simultaneous capacity exists, the two processes can respond more rapidly to changes in customer demand as lead times are reduced.

In cases where the production sequence is important, the connection should also contain agreed rules on how the sequence should be handled, e.g. by changing the sequence so that both processes attain leveled flows. Another scenario is to assure FIFO, i.e. to make sure that the production sequence remains unchanged.

The connection between two processes often, but not always, contains a buffer that creates the necessary disconnection so that the processes will not interfere with each other. In this way the buffer contributes to increasing the actual capacity of each process.

Every connection needs to be updated as conditions change through changed takt, altered work hours, etc. While the workforce has the responsibility to improve the processes, the responsibility to improve the connections between the processes lies with the management. Management has the required overview of the flow and it is logical that they should also have the responsibility to develop and update the connections.

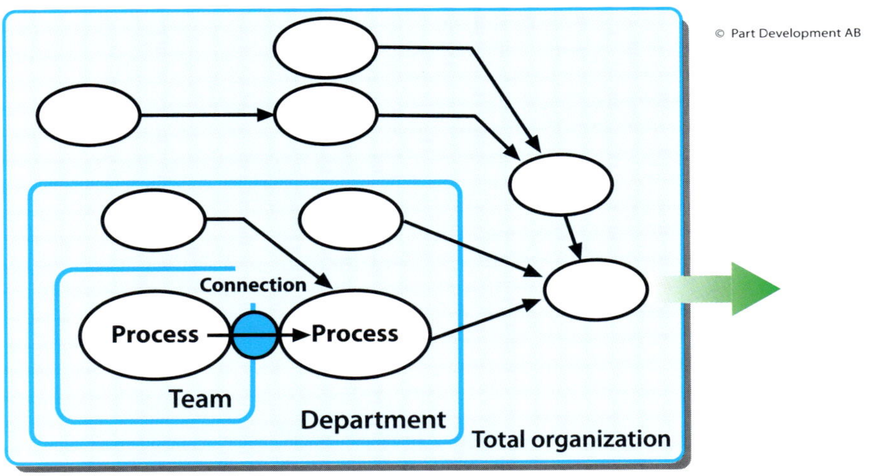

Figure 6-12. *Management and workforce both have improvement responsibility and the improvement work should comprise the processes as well as the connections between them.*

Connection between Processes *Example*

A connection between two processes in a healthcare flow may consist of agreements on how and when patients should be sent from one nursing ward and be received by another, the maximum number of patients that can be received per time unit, under what periods of the day handovers should take place, how information about deviations (e.g. delayed patients) should be communicated, etc.

In an administrative flow it is preferable to define the amount of work the receiving process is permitted to accumulate in its inbox (buffer) before the delivering process temporarily has to stop passing on work tasks. The connection should also include rules for the prioritization of various work tasks or products, i.e. in which sequence they should be processed, and how it can be guaranteed that the desired sequence is maintained throughout the entire administrative flow.

In administration as well as in services and healthcare, decisions concerning capacity are important for the connections between departments, processes and resources. This has to do with decisions concerning what actual capacity each flow part should have, and when work should be carried out in each part of the flow. When work hours in the different parts of the flow do not match, the result is unnecessary waiting time for the product, the customer or the patient, and sometimes also for the members of the workforce.

Order Quantity Limits

For some aspects of a flow there are no rights or wrongs. In these cases standardization entails decision making and agreements with concerned parties on what should be considered normal. An example of an area that may require an agreement is order quantities from customers. When customer demand varies significantly from day to day it entails that the requirements on the supplying processes vary in the same way, and under these circumstances it is difficult to develop efficient flows. How should a process or a flow be designed and dimensioned to be able to cope with all possible scenarios and still be efficient?

To deal with this complex of problems, at least partially, it is often effective to define limits for the size range of orders that can be accepted. It is often claimed that this kind of agreement is impossible to reach with an external customer, and in the cases where the customer does not understand the mutual benefit this is obviously true. In other cases the customer agrees that defining order quantity limits is a common concern. The supplying process benefits from being able to achieve a better balance over time between the allocated resources and the required capacity. This contributes to reducing costs, which may lead to reduced prices. The customer normally also benefits from more reliable deliveries from the supplier, as unreliable deliveries imply considerable extra costs for the customer.

Defining order quantity limits is definitely possible *within* a company. In the company's own value stream there are normally a number of processes that are internal customers. It is common that these internal customers generate unnecessarily large variations in demand rate for the supplying processes to deal with. For the supplier to keep delivery reliability at an acceptable level this kind of behavior is expensive.

In practice order quantity limits function as control levels. When an order is larger than agreed, it is a deviation. In this case the supplying process should inform the customer process and the customer process can then analyze the deviation, find the root cause and find a solution so that the deviation will not recur. The same procedure is applicable when the order quantity is smaller than the lower limit as, given an agreed average order volume, too small order quantities will sooner or later be followed by an order that is too large.

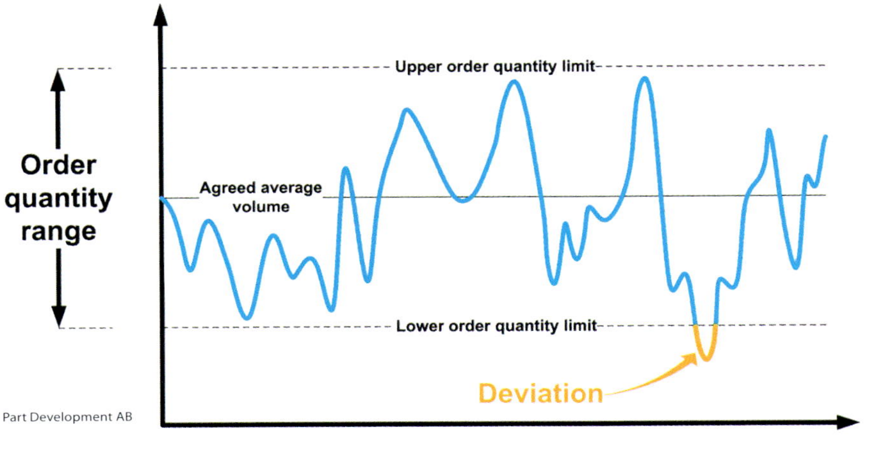

Figure 6-13. *A defined and agreed order quantity range creates possibilities to detect deviations.*

Order Quantity Limits *Example*

An example of applying order quantity limits to non-manufacturing operations is agreeing on the amount of orders, basic purchase data, service customers or patients that are allowed to be passed on to a certain resource per time unit, e.g. per day.

Emergency patients, of course, cannot be treated in this way. They have to be taken care of immediately, if needed. However, to facilitate the planning of an operation it may be wise to question what should really be viewed as immediate needs. It is not unusual that it turns out that the actual customer demand is not as unpredictable as it seems to be.

Successful use of order quantity limits requires successful planning and that everyone involved respects the agreed limits. Investigations have shown that the variation in workload at some surgical wards is higher for planned surgeries than for emergency surgeries. It should of course be the other way round if planning had worked well.

Control Limits for Deviations in Production Quantity

It is a well-known truism that a chain is no stronger than its weakest link. This means, in a value stream context, that the processes in a flow should act within agreed limits so that they do not interfere with each other. An example of such an agreement that has implications for the flow capacity is how much each process is allowed to deviate from the expected production quantity without disturbing the flow.

One way to create conditions propitious to the detection and correction of this type of deviations in time is to define control levels for how large a deviation from the planned production quantity can be before action needs to be taken. By defining control levels and by continuously comparing the actual production quantity (present value) with the expected production quantity (target value), it is possible to take action before the deviations become too extensive. This is, in essence, a way of applying Takt to the processes in a flow.

When the present value reaches the upper control limit this is a signal that the process should be stopped to avoid overproduction. Producing too much in advance is considered to be overproduction which results in unnecessary buffers.

In contrast, when the present value reaches the lower control limit it is a signal that the production backlog is too large in relation to what the flow has been dimensioned to handle. A possible action to take when the lower control limit is reached is to temporarily extend work hours by ordering overtime.

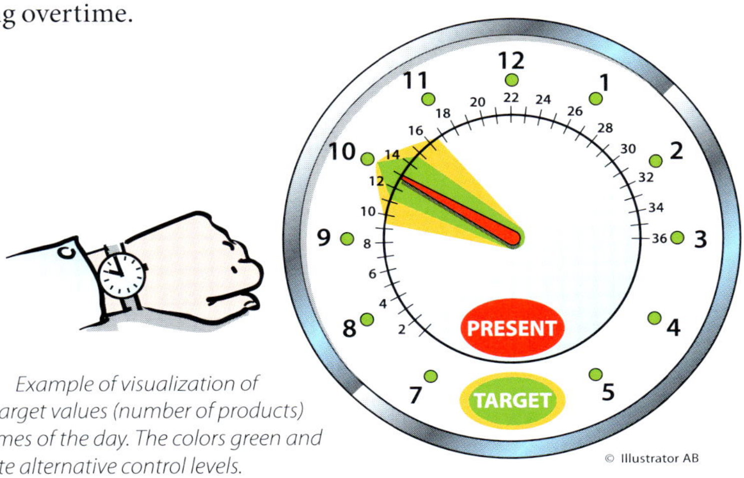

Figure 6-14. *Example of visualization of present and target values (number of products) at different times of the day. The colors green and yellow indicate alternative control levels.*

There is a clear relationship between the normal production quantity range and the required size of the inter-process buffer. A wide range implies that large deviations from the target value are allowed before action is taken, and naturally the buffer has to be dimensioned to handle these large deviations.

Control Levels for Deviations in Production Quantity ***Example***

All operations sometimes proceed faster or slower than planned, e.g. in an automotive service workshop the unexpected sometimes happens which implies that planned service times cannot be met. The cause might be technical and/or organizational. Continuous follow-up of progress according to plan will already at an early stage enable notifying customers that their car will not be ready on time.

Receiving correct information early on is an important part of customer value in services as well as in healthcare. With predefined limits on how much in advance or after the plan activities may lie without having all too severe consequences for the customer, or for other parts of the flow, it is possible to decide what measures should be taken and how the customer should be informed as early as possible.

Buffers

Work in progress (WIP) exists in all flows. These waiting parts or products can be found in more or less well defined intermediate storage spaces along the flow. The term buffer is used in this context to denote a well-defined intermediate storage with a well-defined place and size. Undefined intermediate storage spaces are instead called intermediate storages.

Buffers are of great importance for the performance of a production flow. A buffer's function is to deliver when the process cannot. Buffers are needed partly because of external conditions like customer demand, and partly because of process shortcomings. Within Lean, the goal should be to have as small buffers as possible. They should, however, not be smaller than prevailing conditions allow them to be.

Buffers *Example*

Buffers exist also in non-manufacturing operations. One example is inboxes, which nowadays are usually electronic but sometimes physical piles of paper. Thus, buffers concern tasks waiting to be executed.

A buffer does not have to be electronic or physical, it can also consist of time. Time buffers are common in flows where certain activities go on for a longer period of time, such as project work. In this case it is common that the project time schedule contains time buffers to handle uncertainties about the duration of the various project activities.

In many production flows intermediate storage spaces have emerged without proper thought. Their sizes have often been determined by the space available at the storage location or on the floor. In addition, they have not been adjusted in accordance to changes in production volume or when problems have either emerged or been dealt with.

A buffer should be there to serve one or more purposes, i.e. one single buffer can simultaneously serve a number of different purposes. The following buffer functions (each of them serving a specific purpose) can be distinguished:

- Disturbance buffer
- Buffer for planned stops
- Consumption buffer
- Sequence buffer

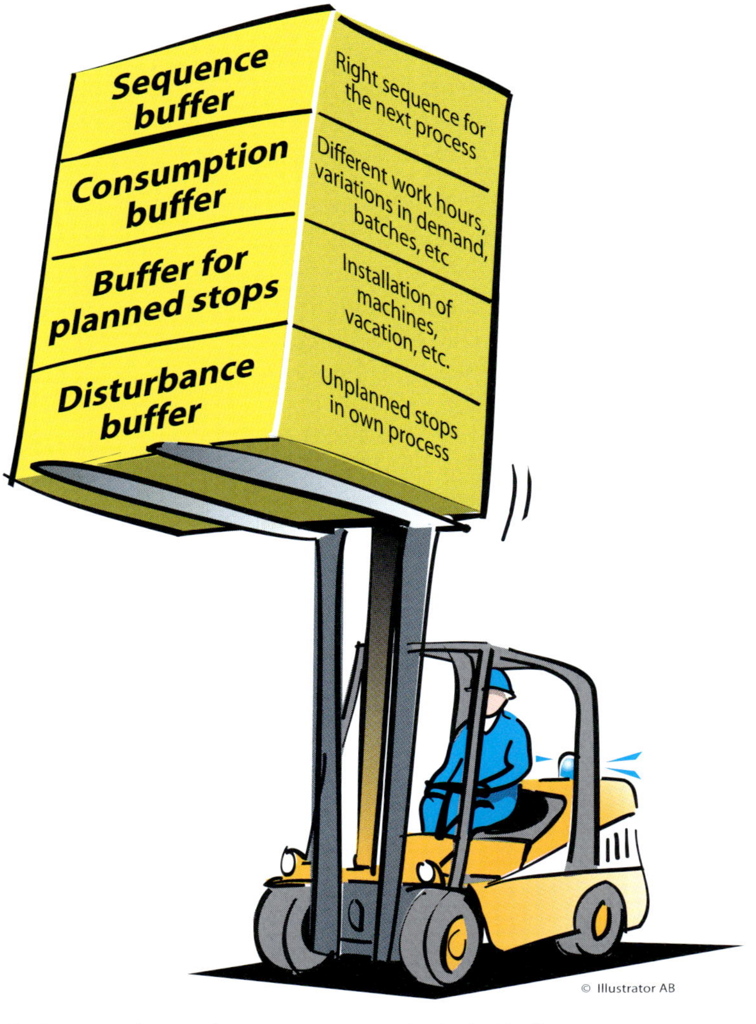

Figure 6-15. *Buffer functions that can be present in one single physical buffer.*

The function of the disturbance buffer is to cover the unplanned stops that occur in a process. In practice, this buffer function exists in all buffers as all processes suffer from unplanned stops to a major or minor extent. In order to be able to dimension the disturbance buffer, the characteristics of the stops must be known. The length of the stops for which the buffer is dimensioned should have been defined. Knowledge of the characteristics of the stops means detailed knowledge about the stops in terms of number and duration.

It is irrational to dimension a buffer to cover any problem that might surface in a process. Instead, it should be dimensioned based on a judgment of what stops can be expected and on a decision on acceptable risk and cost. This is basically the same discussion as when a house is to be insured. A person who is absolutely sure that nothing harmful will happen to his/her house would probably be prepared to accept a high excess. However, should there be a high risk of burglary, it may be sensible to pay the extra for a low excess and invest in a burglar alarm.

To be able to make the right decision on what the disturbance buffer should cope with, detailed knowledge about the unplanned stops is required. Are there a lot of short stops, or a small number of long stops? From a disturbance buffer point of view, many small stops are preferable. This, because a smaller disturbance buffer will provide sufficient delivery reliability, as the buffer level will not drop substantially before the buffer is refilled.

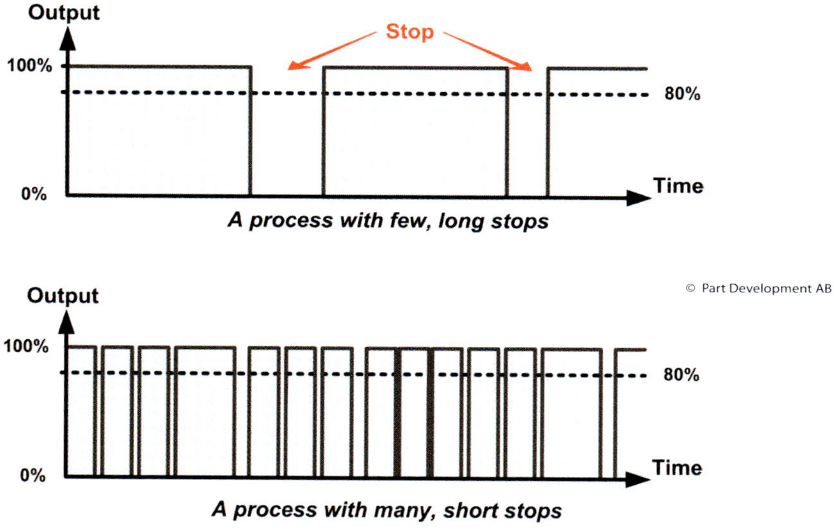

Figure 6-16. *Example of processes having the same total stop time but different stop characteristics.*

The disturbance buffer is the part of a buffer that, together with the sequence buffer, provides the safety level which is the absolute minimum buffer level. The actual safety provided by a given size of the disturbance buffer depends on the takt. If the takt increases, the disturbance buffer also needs to be increased so that a constant level of safety against stops in the flow is maintained.

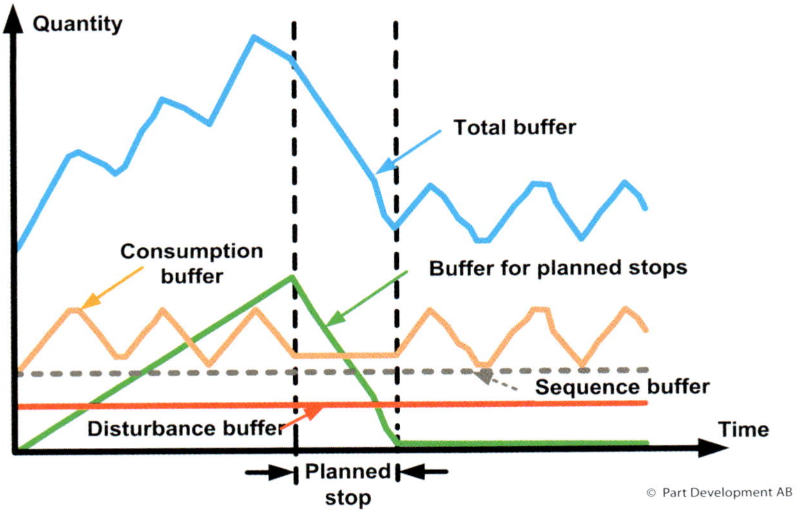

Figure 6-17. *Ideal characteristics of each buffer function.*

Disturbance Buffer — *Example*

A disturbance buffer in an administrative flow can either be a time buffer, i.e. extra time for e.g. producing a tender or basic salary data, or an electronic buffer where products are stored in some information system while waiting to be delivered at the correct time.

The need for disturbance buffers in non-manufacturing operations exists for exactly the same reasons as in manufacturing operations. It is a certainty that something will happen that causes delays. It might be information systems going down. Therefore, to make sure that salary payments are not delayed it may be prudent to produce the basic salary data some time in advance, and then pay out the money on the right day. To get a permanent reduction of the time buffer, operational improvements are needed, e.g. increased efficiency in information system support.

Detailed knowledge on stop characteristics is also necessary in non-manufacturing operations so that the disturbance buffer can be correctly dimensioned. What knowledge do we have about the number and duration of information system stops, about how long a surgical ward has to wait for delayed patients, etc? These are questions that may be difficult to answer, but such information would support buffer dimensioning decisions.

Unlike the case with the disturbance buffer, the buffer for planned stops varies naturally over time. This part of the buffer is built prior to the planned stop, so that it will be in place for e.g. a stop for planned maintenance. Then, after the stop is realized, the buffer size is reduced through deliveries to the customer process with no concurrent replenishment from the supplying process.

Planned Stops — *Example*

Planned stops due to absence such as vacation, training and conferences exist in all kinds of operations, and they obviously need to be somehow dealt with. In non-manufacturing operations, where there is no possibility of storing products, it may be handled by rescheduling to increase capacity during a period before and after the planned stop.

The consumption buffer similarly varies in size over time. These variations are normally more frequent than the variations in the buffer for planned stops. A consumption buffer is needed between two processes that are not synchronized, i.e. not simultaneous. For example, a consumption buffer is required between two processes with different work hours. In this case the buffer need is determined by the fact that the two processes do not supply and deliver simultaneously. The same problem occurs when processes produce in batch sizes larger than one. Here, some products are in fact not demanded until later but they are produced in advance to fill out the batch. Thus, these products obviously need to be stored until they are needed.

Variations in customer demand also call for a consumption buffer. In flows with defined order quantity ranges, a buffer is still needed because even if the supplying process is leveled, the customer process is not. The size of the consumption buffer should be adapted to the size of the order quantity range. A large order quantity range allows for large variations in customer demand and therefore a large consumption buffer is required.

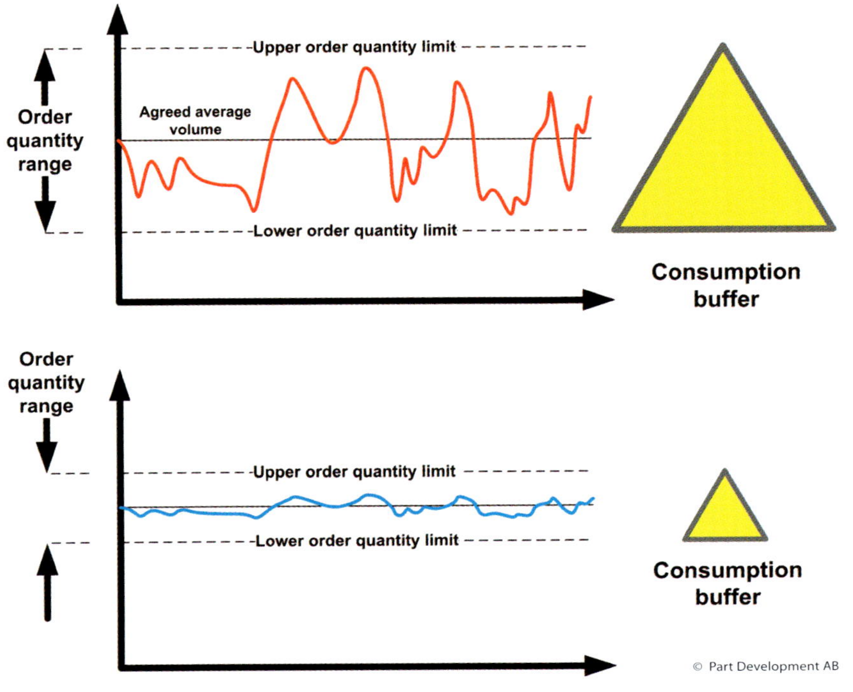

Figure 6-18. *The relation between order quantity range and the need for a consumption buffer.*

Consumption Buffer *Example*

In some processing operations a certain type of applications may be processed on only one day of the week. However, the applications arrive continuously during the week and they are stored in a consumption buffer waiting to be processed.

In an order office the orders do not normally arrive at a smooth rate. However, the capacity to process orders is normally constant during all weekdays. This implies that some orders will be kept waiting in a consumption buffer. The question is how large this consumption buffer should be allowed to become until a decision on e.g. adding resources must be taken. In this case demand amplitude variations and the order office's promised delivery time to its customers are important parameters in the dimensioning of the consumption buffer.

A sequence buffer may be required when the production sequence is important for the flow. Here, the production sequence either needs to be restored in order to satisfy the customer, or changed to provide optimal conditions for the flow. A sequence buffer is a number of available products that can be rearranged so that the desired production sequence can be restored or created. The sequence buffer should, analogously to the disturbance buffer, be constant in size over time. The sequence buffer provides a part of the total buffer's safety level.

Sequence Buffer *Example*

Basic purchasing data are normally produced in the sequence that is most efficient for purchasing and product development. However, when it is time to contact suppliers it is preferable to discuss all purchasing matters with a certain supplier at one and the same time. Thus, the basic purchasing data is produced in one sequence and used in another. This means that the data have to be stored in a sequence buffer that permits rearranging the sequence.

Planning and Control of the Value Stream

Planning and control have a major impact on the performance of the value stream. The main principle Just-In-Time (JIT) states that the flow should be controlled by an actual demand signal, i.e. by actual customer demand. However, it does not necessarily mean that all activities are triggered by real orders from an end customer. When the lead time is longer than the agreed delivery time, this is not even possible.

Therefore, consumption-controlled production in many cases entails that processes are triggered by an actual demand signal from the next process step, i.e. from the next internal customer. To make consumption-controlled production work in practice, it is important that the available resources are not overloaded, i.e. that the demand rate is not higher than the actual capacity. Of course, this is equally important in a traditional flow but the problem is usually more visible in an efficient flow that reveals deviations.

Overloading a production system will result in problems for the customer as well as for the internal organization. The customer suffers in terms of late deliveries and the internal organization is subjected to overstrain, overtime, rescheduling, etc. The same kind of problems can be found in administration, services and healthcare.

Planning

Planning plays an important role in creating the necessary conditions for controlling an operation by an actual demand signal. The primary tasks of the planning activity in an operation striving for Lean are the following:

- Plan the operation so that the customer order load in the production system does not exceed its actual capacity
- Plan the operation so that the customer order load in the production is constant over days, shifts, etc. (i.e. leveling of production volume)
- Plan the production sequence in a way that products and variants with large work content are distributed as evenly as possible over the production sequence (i.e. leveling of work content)

To load the production system up to the desired level is of course only possible if this level is known. The desired level is equal to the actual capacity of the limiting resource, i.e. the process in the flow with the lowest actual capacity.

Planning ***Example***

Planning is an important prerequisite for achieving high efficiency irrespective of the kind of work. In e.g. a surgical ward planning influences work satisfaction, patient satisfaction, as well as the ward's actual capacity. The key to accomplish effective planning is to have detailed knowledge about capacity and to understand what kind of measures can be taken to improve leveling.

A problem in non-manufacturing operations is that they often lack time data. This implies that it is difficult for the planning function to provide a proper plan. However, there are examples in e.g. healthcare where surgical operations are planned using time data based on experience at the individual level. In this case, in spite of the desire to apply standardized work, it may be considered justified to use individual time data as surgery times normally differ significantly between surgeons, although they hopefully perform the surgical operations in the same standardized way.

Deviations occur in all processes which entails that planned production times will also have deviations. As this is known, it should be accounted for in the planning activity. If it is known that process efficiency in a certain process is 80 per cent, it means that the process can only deliver acceptable products 80 per cent of the planned production time. During the rest of the planned production time, the process suffers from disturbances such as quality problems or unplanned stops. It would then not be rational to load the production system with orders to a total workload corresponding to 100 per cent of the planned production time. Nevertheless, this is the default procedure in many companies, and it results in daily production backlogs. Problems arise in the flow and the whole situation seems to be hopeless since there is never a realistic possibility for the workforce to actually "win the game".

In the example above no more than 80 per cent of the planned production time should be filled with orders. The remaining 20 per cent will constitute a restoration time, i.e. time to catch up with the actual production backlog.

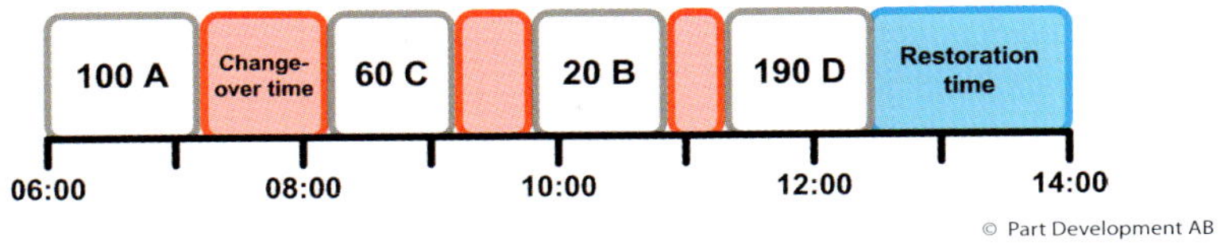

Figure 6-19. *Visual planning where the restoration time is placed at the end of the time interval. A-D refer to different products.*

When this production plan is put into practice, a number of unplanned stops will occur entailing that production will consume more time than planned. Therefore, restoration time will be needed so that the production backlog will be eliminated before the end of the shift. As the size of the restoration time is based on averaged information, it is normal that the entire restoration time will be used in order to complete all the orders that had been planned to be produced during the shift.

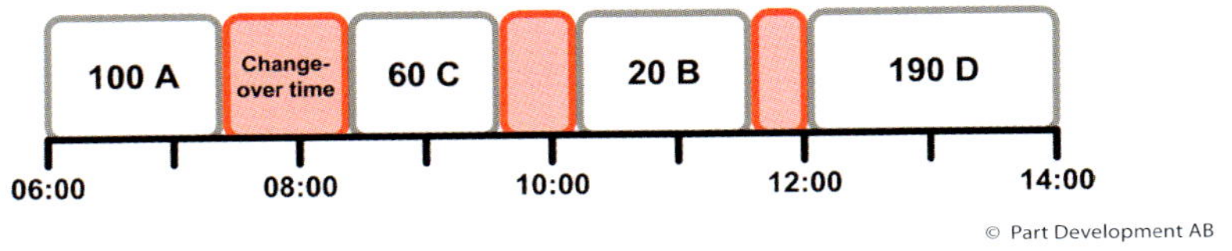

Figure 6-20. *Production result showing how every product has consumed more production time than what was planned for. Thus, the entire restoration time was needed.*

Introducing restoration time might seem to imply lower capacity, but that is not the case. Capacity is not affected, and in fact the only difference is that the flow will not become overloaded. The capacity of the flow will remain unchanged until positive actions are taken to increase it.

Restoration time will improve delivery reliability. More orders than the flow is able to cope with on the average will not be planned, and if a production backlog were to appear, it can be kept at a manageable level. Thus, the restoration time reduces the need for repeated reschedulings due to production backlogs.

Restoration time is there to restore the production situation by eliminating the production backlog. If, in an extreme case, the restoration time would be scheduled once yearly, there would probably be an enormous production backlog. To eliminate this backlog would require enormous resources during the process restoration time. Furthermore, very large buffers would be required as they would have to make up for production losses during almost a year before being refilled. In customer order production this scenario is not possible unless the agreed delivery times are very long.

To avoid the just discussed, restoration time should be planned in as often as possible, ideally into every shift. In this way deviations from the planned production situation will be as small as possible, and the workforce will have a fair chance of producing what is expected during the shift.

The size of the restoration time is based on averaged data. Hence, on those occasions when production experiences more than the average amount of problems, the restoration time will not be long enough. The production backlog that is then created should be prioritized in the next planning interval, e.g. the next shift or the next day. In cases where the production problems are smaller than average, i.e. the actual time for unplanned stops is shorter than average, there will be excess time. There is then the possibility to decide if the excess time should be spent on improvement work, or if orders for the next planning interval should be produced in advance. It should be noted that the latter choice is a form of overproduction, that is, a form of waste.

Restoration Time ***Example***

Restoration time in non-manufacturing operations can be viewed as a kind of time buffer expressed in concrete times, where use of the time buffer is actively followed up so that deviations can be detected. Each time restoration time is used is considered a deviation.

From the description of restoration time it follows that e.g. a service technician should not book customer visits for all of his/her work hours. A certain part of the time, e.g. at the end of the day, should be unbooked restoration time, which would normally not be used. In this way, the need to spend time rescheduling customer visits a number of days ahead is reduced. Rescheduling customer visits to be able to catch up adds no customer value, but rather annoys the customers.

By avoiding this kind of non-value-adding work, planning restoration time into the schedule should not decrease capacity, although it might seem so at the planning stage. It is, however, important to emphasize that process efficiency must be known in order to dimension the restoration time properly. Too little restoration time will make it difficult to handle customer demand, while too much restoration time, i.e. too much space in the schedule, will decrease capacity.

Production Control

A flow should be consumption-controlled and easy to control. A simple and unambiguous way to create a pull system based on actual demand signals is basically all that is needed. However, success in this requires that the standardized solutions in the flow are good enough. Defining and improving all the standards in a flow requires extensive, time consuming work. Still, it is a necessary first step. Introducing an actual demand signal, by using e.g. Kanban or buffer control, will not bring the desired effects unless the underlying flow works sufficiently well.

Introducing a simple method to transfer the demand signal does not take long, but should nonetheless be viewed as the crowning glory. The major challenge is to improve the production flow to a level where the positive effects of improved production control can be realized. As a simple rule of thumb, about 90 per cent of the effort is spent defining and improving the standards in the flow, and only about 10 per cent needs to be used in linking actual demand signals to the flow.

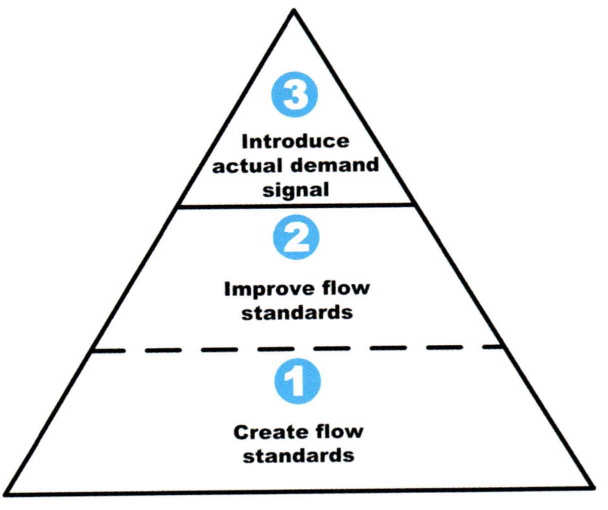

Figure 6-21. *Necessary steps to achieve the desired effects from improved production control.*

Actual Demand Signal ***Example***

In healthcare the actual demand signal may be signaling that a nursing ward is ready to receive a patient from another ward. Simple signal systems can be used to clarify when the receiving ward is ready. It may be accomplished by such simple means as floor markings with adhesive tape where an empty square on the floor signals that another bed may be rolled in. When all squares are occupied the delivering ward will have to wait to transfer the patient since it has received a clear signal that there are problems ahead in the flow. In cases where the different nursing wards are located at different levels of the building, the same information can be supplied by e.g. light signals.

The alternative to such a pull system would be a situation where the delivering nursing ward sends the patient no matter what the situation is like at the receiving end. In this case the consequence may be that the receiving ward's problems (when it cannot catch up) will increase with the increasing number of patients to take care of. In addition, the deviation will not be noticed to the same extent.

Strive for a Perfect State

No matter how good or bad the standardized solutions in the flow are, they can always be improved. This mindset entails striving for perfection and is represented by the roof of the Lean model. Even with high ambitions, it will often be too complex and resource demanding to simultaneously try to improve all production flows in a factory. It is normally prudent to start small (a pilot flow) and focus on *one* product family and have the ambition to turn it into a very good flow that complies with Lean principles as far as possible. A successful pilot flow normally helps to make the rest of the organization understand what the Lean principles mean in practice. This will in turn create a desire among the members of the workforce to likewise improve the other flows. Important criteria in the choice of a pilot flow are that it should:

- Not be too complex
- Lead to visible and measurable results
- Be a good arena for learning

Achieving a perfect flow and a well-balanced pull system at the very beginning is utopian. The most effective way to proceed in that direction is to improve in small and controlled steps. At every step it is important to analyze the results from the previous step, and to learn and reflect in order to succeed in the further improvements on the path towards the perfect (unattainable) system.

A possible reason why the work on improving value streams is not always successful is that key persons have not been involved. The value stream is the arena for the improvement work, but all too often management is not present. Management has to *lead* the work of detecting and eliminating waste. The only way to do that is by entering the arena and taking an active part and interest in the improvement work.

As has been stated many times previously, striving for Lean is not a project that has an end; it is instead a continuous improvement process. Organizations that stop this continuous improvement work run the risk of being overtaken by their competitors.

The difference between Lean and more traditional ways of running an operation is that there is a different view on how good results are created.

7. Towar

Towards the Goal

In an operation striving for Lean the consistent application of agreed methods is crucial. There is a conviction that the desired result will come when the right methods are applied in the correct way. This emphasis on method does not mean that the results are unimportant, it is just another way of viewing how good results are created.

Problems with Traditional Financial Control

A good financial result is a necessity for the long-term survival of any organization and it should naturally be carefully tracked. In this sense there is no difference between traditional organizations and organizations that have come far on their journey towards Lean. However, problems may arise when an organization striving for Lean is calculating and tracking results using methods common in traditional operations. This is the background to the development of *Lean Accounting*. The term does not refer to any new financial system; it rather denotes transferring the Lean thoughts to the financial department, thereby creating a financial control system that is aligned with what the organization wants to achieve.

Understanding of the differences between Lean and more traditional ways of carrying out operations is required from everyone all the way up to the board of directors. Otherwise there is a risk that a department manager striving for Lean will end up on a collision course with the board of directors' demands for rapid results. It may take a long time to achieve results, but this is not always the case. The length of time it will take to achieve successful and long-term lasting results from the Lean effort depends on the company's current situation, its willingness and ability to change, and its drive. In this respect, there are naturally large differences between different organizations. For some of these the first year with Lean is solely characterized by the education of personnel and by minor improvements that do not bring noticeable effects to the financial result. This may of course result in frustration and if the decision makers lack the right understanding the risk is imminent that the effort will be shut down.

Large-scale Thinking is Encouraged

A fundamental problem with traditional financial controls is that they tend to drive organizations towards decisions that are not effective from a holistic perspective. This is true e.g. in the choice of batch sizes. Traditional financial control is based on an outlook where large volumes and economies of scale prevail. Trying to reduce waste by producing in smaller batch sizes is difficult in such an environment. The following example illustrates this problem:

Cost Calculation *Example*

Traditional calculation of the manufacturing cost of a certain part includes a change-over cost that is based on time consumption and the cost of the machine. The cost is divided between the number of parts that are produced in each batch.

Having a change-over cost of $100 and a batch size of 500 parts will result in a change-over cost per unit of 20 cents. Reducing the batch size to 200 parts will increase the change-over cost to 50 cents per unit.

According to this calculation model larger batches imply cheaper parts but, as mentioned earlier, in the long term using smaller batches is a way of reducing waste, and thus costs, in the flow. The problem with large batch sizes is that they normally lead to an increase of other costs such as cost of unsalability, cost of poor quality, cost of facilities, and cost of tied-up capital. In addition, improvement work is complicated by the fact that large batch sizes require large buffers. Buffers hide waste – they prevent deviations from being detected since the initial problems in the flow are dealt with by the buffer. Buffers in themselves also create waste in the form of unnecessary handling, unnecessary transports, etc. This is problematic as detecting and eliminating waste is the actual core of Lean.

Traditional financial control encourages the utilization of expensive investment objects around the clock irrespective of actual customer demand. It is assumed that the equipment in this way generates more revenues relative to its cost. However, within Lean the goal is to use an investment only when the customer demand is there. This is just another example of how the two approaches clash in practice.

In healthcare the desire to optimize the utilization of expensive equipment has led to the centralization of some functions. Radiotherapy is one typical example of this. Patients queuing to the radiotherapy department come from a large number of nursing wards, which all send X-ray referrals independently of each other. With a high and steady workload and high volumes this will probably imply that the cost per performed X-ray is low. At the same time a large number of care chains are broken which results in an unnecessarily large amount of expensive beds being occupied for an unnecessarily long time in many different nursing wards. Thus, there is definitely reason to believe that the increase in nursing costs is higher than the decrease in costs at the radiotherapy department. This is the result of focusing on optimizing a specific function instead of the entire flow.

Within Lean there is an endeavor to utilize resources so that company results improve at the overall level but not necessarily in every specific department. Organizations that aim to make sure that everyone is busy, irrespective of current customer demand, will find it difficult to increase their profit margins. This approach often leads to overproduction which in turn implies increased tied-up capital, longer lead times, increased unsalability, increased material handling, etc. The challenge is to find a way to level production in order to reach a stable and high utilization of resources at the same time as production is made to follow customer demand.

The View of Revenues and Costs

The view on how revenues and costs can be steered has an impact on a company's endeavor to strive for Lean. Companies have traditionally often calculated product prices based on existing costs.

Cost + Profit = Sales price

Such a view does not automatically support a way of working that is aimed at reducing costs through the elimination of waste. Cost is instead largely considered to be a fixed parameter and the desired profit margin will then determine the selling price.

In an increasingly competitive environment there is the risk that this approach will reduce competitiveness. For this reason in Lean the product price is considered to be set by the market.

Market price – Costs = Profit

Today, many large industrial customers set a target price, i.e. a price that they are willing to pay. If the work on reducing costs is not successful enough, the result is that the supplier may have to reduce his profit margin in order to remain a potential supplier. This gives a far stronger incentive to reduce waste in an operation. The automotive industry, which has been experiencing tough competition for many years, adopted target pricing quite a long time ago.

Focusing on reducing costs often has the positive side effect of a better overview of costs for the organization. Improved cost control will moreover reduce the risk of miscalculation in the quotation process.

Evaluation of Capacity

Given a constant demand rate, a systematic reduction of waste will sooner or later result in a situation where there is excess capacity. If this situation is solved by dismissing redundant staff, costs will of course be reduced but at the same time the first step to killing the improvement work will have been taken. Who would want to continue to put effort into improving the operations when the consequence is that you or some of your colleagues become redundant?

Thus, narrow focus on cost reduction is obviously not the right path to take; instead the approach should be to utilize the increased efficiency by increasing sales. In that way the important improvement work that is the key to long-term success can be maintained. The excess capacity that arises from a rationalization is a freed resource that can be utilized to expand the business. Without reducing profits, the freed capacity can be used to take new market share through aggressive pricing. The capacity required for the new activities has already been paid for by the improvement work that has been performed. With the new market share there is the possibility to continue the new activities even when operating at prevailing market price levels. This will in turn increase profits.

However, in order to engage in the right business activities it is necessary to value capacity correctly. This is illustrated by the following example.

Evaluation of Capacity ***Example***

An operator's task at a certain machining operation is to load parts into the machine and to unload the parts once they have been processed. The cycle time of the machine is five minutes and given the short cycle time it is difficult to find additional work tasks that the operator can perform while waiting for the machine.

Let us say that 480 parts per week are produced. The customer asks if it is possible to add a manual task that takes about three minutes. For this extra work the customer is willing to pay $5 per product. When the financial department evaluates this offer, including various additional costs, change-over costs, etc., they find that the cost to execute the task is $8. Thus, a sales price below $8 will produce a loss. Their demand for this higher price resulted in the company losing this additional business.

The question is whether the company would actually have made a loss accepting a price of $5. Depending on how you calculate you will come to different conclusions. From a Lean perspective, the operator is already paid for and the waiting time during the machine's cycle time is waste. Thus, having the opportunity to decrease this waste cannot be unprofitable. If the company could get $5 extra per product it would imply a yearly financial contribution of more than $100 000.

An alternative to switching freed capacity to work on new orders is to utilize the excess capacity to accelerate the improvement work. The results of the improvements will shorten production times and this extra time can then be used to make even more improvements. This will not directly affect the financial result, as increased capacity in a situation where there already is excess capacity will hardly generate new revenues in the short term. However, it will bring the possibility to be even better prepared to take on new orders, thereby increasing profits in the long run.

Measuring Performance

An organization striving for Lean needs to be evaluated and reviewed in a manner that is in accordance with the Lean way of thinking. Performance evaluations play an important role in motivating the workforce to do the right things. The evaluation process must send the right signals. People want to be appreciated for what they do and consequently they will act in a way that will produce good results when measured by the prevailing performance evaluation method. If management verbally promotes Lean but continues to evaluate and review the operation in the same way as before, people in the organization will revert to the traditional way of working because this is what management seems to appreciate most.

Connection to Improvement Work

Financial performance evaluation at an aggregate level may be difficult to break down to a level that is relevant to the workforce. If the information is not broken down it cannot be used in the improvement work. It will be difficult for the workforce to understand what needs to be done to achieve the overall goals. A combination of financial and non-financial performance indicators is normally preferable. Financial performance indicators are obviously important for external accounting, but non-financial indicators are better suited for the workforce running the operations.

A DuPont chart can be used to make people understand how various improvement activities contribute to the financial performance indicators. The DuPont chart displays what affects the company's overall and long-term goals. The DuPont chart comprises all the three components of profitability:

- Revenues
- Costs
- Capital

Therefore it is a suitable way to present the concrete effects of improvements in the operations.

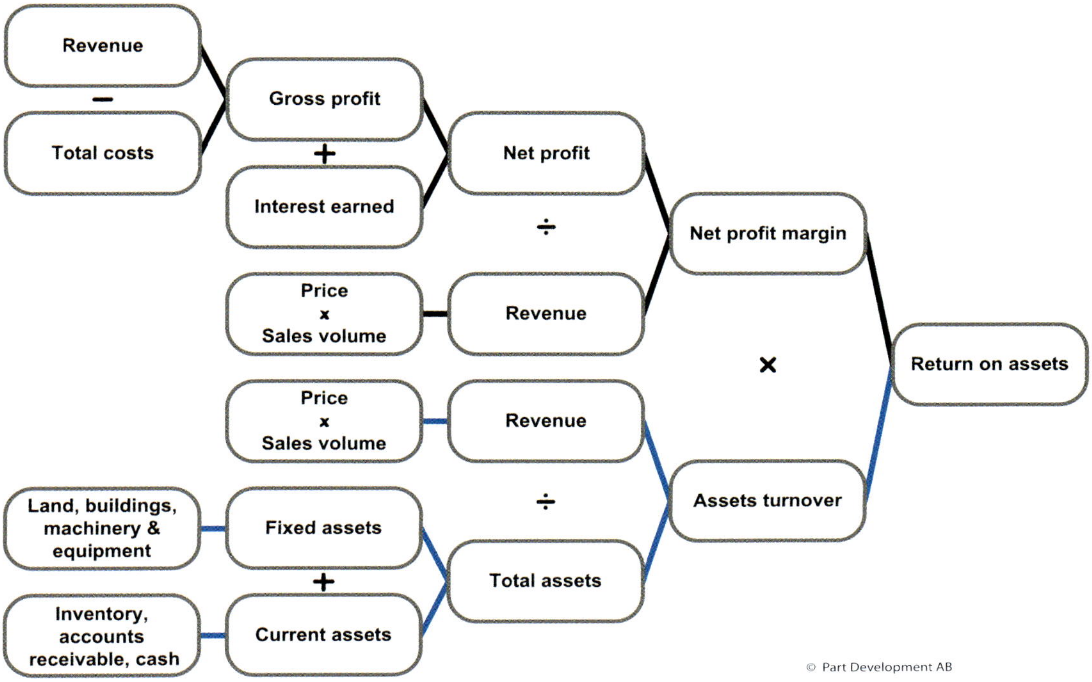

Figure 7-1. *DuPont chart.*

A number of relationships can be made clear by the DuPont chart. To achieve as high a return on assets as possible, the net profit margin and the assets turnover should be maximized. The upper half of the DuPont chart shows that a high net profit margin is based on a high gross profit. Gross profit is defined as:

Gross profit = Revenue – Total costs

The connection between Lean and cost reduction is obvious. Eliminating waste, and thereby costs, in small and controlled steps is the actual core of Lean. However, it is normally difficult to predict to what extent Lean will affect revenues. When the market price cannot be changed, sales volumes must increase if revenues are to increase. Is this possible? Yes, a successful Lean effort definitely gives customer benefits in the form of improved quality, improved delivery reliability, shorter delivery times, etc. This will create opportunities for increasing customer demand.

A successful Lean effort moreover increases actual capacity and this new capacity can be used to take on new orders which, if the company succeeds in selling the products, will increase revenues without increasing costs commensurately.

The lower half of the DuPont chart shows what affects the assets turnover. Lean has implications also in this case. The assets turnover is defined as:

Assets turnover = Revenue / Total assets

Reliable and predictable processes in combination with efficient flows create conditions for reducing buffers without decreasing delivery reliability. Thus the tied-up capital in the flow (current assets) is reduced and consequently so are the total assets. The result is an increased assets turnover.

The financial goals indicate the company's desired direction, but to have the right impact on the organization they should be broken down to concrete performance indicators at the workforce level. Only those parameters that people can influence should be reviewed at this level. Visualizing e.g. the amount of tied-up capital in central storage will probably not influence the workers' way of working, as it is too difficult for them to see the relationship between their work and the inventory levels in central storage. The review process should therefore be broken down in a way that makes it easier to understand how a specific department should act in order to reduce tied-up capital. Within one department this might be reducing change-over times so as to be able to reduce batch sizes, which in turn creates the proper conditions for reducing the storage. Another department should perhaps be focusing on improving quality so that, in the long run, it would be possible to diminish the central storage. Thus, to be able to make proper breakdowns of the performance indicators it is necessary to understand and analyze the entire flow.

In some cases it is necessary to discuss company-wide financial performance indicators with the entire staff. The members of the workforce need to be e.g. continuously updated about the financial result of the company. This is important as their financial security lies in that of the company. In these situations, the company-wide performance indicators are not a problem as long as they are correctly explained to the workforce. However, presenting numbers like these without commenting them, and refraining from linking the results to the work performed may send the wrong signals. This is illustrated by the following example.

Cause and Effect *Example*

A manufacturing company purchases materials and sells their products on the international market. The company has adopted the Lean way of thinking and the importance of applying the agreed ways of working is continuously emphasized to the manufacturing workforce.

On one occasion the company made a financial loss even though operational performance had been better than ever before. The reason for the poor financial result was that the company had made large currency losses. Thus, it had nothing to do with the performance of the manufacturing personnel.

In this example there was nothing wrong with the method or the workers' way of applying the method. This kind of information must be clearly pointed out to the workforce so that they do not start questioning their ways of working.

Involve the Workforce

In Lean, processes and flows are measured instead of people, but there is no general answer to exactly *what* should be measured. The important thing is that the performance indicators bring something to the operation and that there is a clear connection to the whole. The workforce must be able to understand how the performance indicators are related to each other and how they can be influenced. To deeply involve all employees in the measurement of performance they should be invited to participate when performance indicators are defined. When only management is interested in performance indicators and reviews, there will be no commitment by the workforce. Thus, production reviews play an important role in supporting the Lean effort. The motivation to do a good job as well as the choice of improvement activities are affected by how the operation is evaluated and reviewed.

There are a large number of common performance indicators to choose from, and in order to make the right choice it is important to identify who should be supported by a certain performance indicator. Examples of financial performance indicators are assets turnover, profit margin and return on assets. Performance indicators of this kind are important for external accounting and should therefore be measured regardless of whether the company is striving for Lean or not. Non-financial performance indicators supporting Lean instead focus on waste at a concrete level and are thus clearly related to the workers' activities. Examples are quality, lead time, process efficiency and work environment.

A performance indicator can in turn be computed in a number of different ways, but it is important that the performance indicators are relevant and easy for everyone to understand. From a simple review, everyone should be able to understand the goal and the present situation without the need for any deeper knowledge of statistics or economics.

The review results should also be easily available and be presented simply and graphically. A simple diagram with the current situation and some historical facts is a good example. The trend in the result is often the most interesting fact, and by focusing more on the trend than on the measured value, it is easier to send the signal that continuous improvements in small steps are preferable to large revolutionary changes. To further accentuate the information in a diagram it can include color markings indicating the trend during the last measurement period.

A good way to improve the accessibility of important information is to display it at the place of work, e.g. on a board at a central location. In this way it becomes natural for the employees to show their results during external visits or visits from other departments. The pride that many people experience in showing their good results to others brings motivation that should not be underestimated.

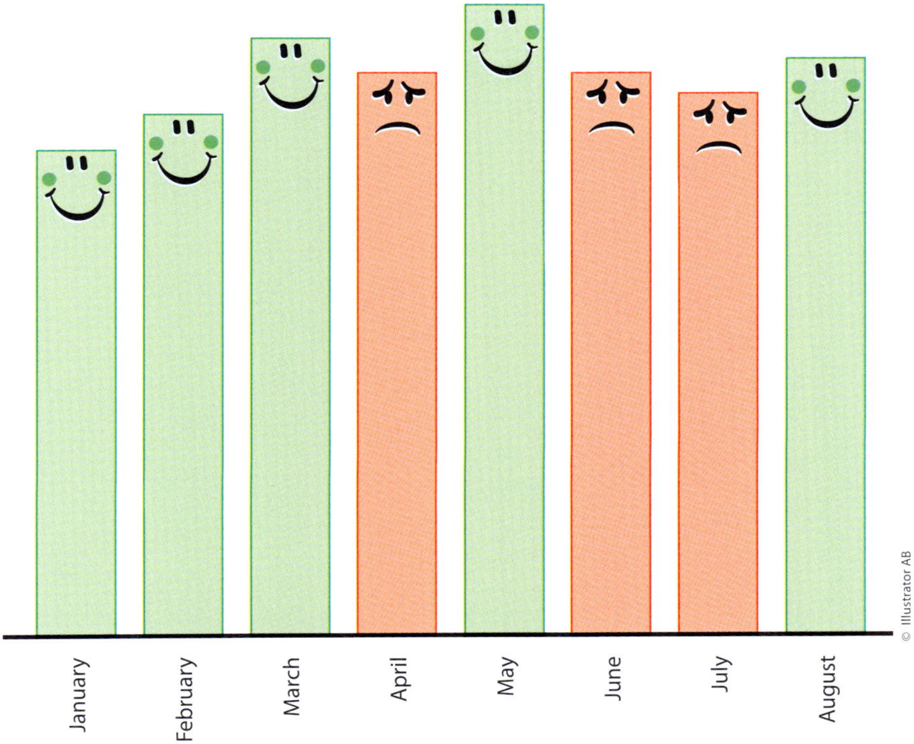

Figure 7-2. *The trend of the results can be visualized by simple means.*

Review Frequency

What the appropriate review frequency in a specific case should be depends largely on how much effort is required to gather the data. In general, the more frequent the feedback the better. This is because data very rapidly become out of date and recent information is more valuable to the improvement work. Therefore, from a theoretical perspective, reviews should be made as frequently as possible. However, a very intensive review schedule may in practice decrease productivity, as a lot of resources will be tied up in data collection and reviewing instead of adding value in the operation.

The more frequently an operation is reviewed, the earlier deviations can be detected, and this will in turn make it easier to find the root cause of each deviation. The moment the deviation occurs, the possibilities of finding clues to its cause are at their highest. This is also the reason why the Aviation Board of Accident Investigation strives to investigate an accident as soon as possible. The sooner they can investigate the scene of the accident, the better are the possibilities of finding the cause of the accident. Some important clues and evidence may be more difficult to come by and analyze as time passes.

Figure 7-3. *The Aviation Board of Accident Investigation strives for a rapid and detailed collection of facts in order to increase the possibilities of finding the root cause of the accident.*

By e.g. measuring process efficiency once a week, an organization will find out how good or bad a process or a flow has been on average during this week. However, this low review frequency will make it very difficult to understand the *reasons* why process efficiency was lower than 100 per cent. Major machine breakdowns are often easy to remember even after some time has passed, but it is barely possible to get a grip on those small stops and disturbances that are usually relatively easily dealt with. It is not until it is known *exactly* what caused the deviations that they can be resolved. To get this kind of specific information it is crucial that stops and disturbances are noted *instantly* as they occur.

In a flow where Takt is strictly applied, reviews are made with the frequency given by the takt time, i.e. when the product moves to the succeeding operation. The review is constituted by checking whether all process steps have been accomplished thus making delivery to the next process step possible. This can be compared to a minor closing of accounts at the end of the takt time. In this way everyone is aware of how they are doing in relation to the production plan, as this is directly connected to the stop time.

Another benefit of frequent reviews is that they make it clear to everyone that time is always important. If a flow, where Takt is not applied, is only reviewed every Friday afternoon there is a great risk that a stop that took place Monday morning is not considered a big problem. People often tend to think that the rest of the week is available to catch up production and eliminate the backlog. Thus, more frequent reviews make it easier for everyone to see the root cause and consequences of every stop.

Success is Created from Deviations

In this chapter it has been pointed out that financial control as well as performance indicators have a major impact on an organization striving for Lean. It cannot be stressed too much that results are also very important for an organization striving for Lean. The difference here between Lean and more traditional ways of running an operation is that there is a different view on how good results are created. There are better ways to reach success than to exclusively strive for economies of scale and to control activities to ensure good short-term values of the overall financial performance indicators. The difficulty of estimating in advance what will be achieved by a Lean effort implies that some decisions need to be based on a conviction that it is the right way to go, instead of always requiring a positive business case.

The work of detecting and resolving deviations is fundamental for achieving good results in all organizations. Performance indicators play an important role in encouraging the organization to work on deviations. The commitment of all employees is crucial in this work and is based on an understanding and acceptance of the performance indicators used to guide the organization towards its goal. Involving people and breaking down performance indicators to concrete levels are matters of major importance.

Changing an entire organization's way of relating to operations is a change of mindset that takes time and requires that management is convinced and persistent.

8. Cross

Crossroad Thoughts

To strive for Lean means to choose a path that requires conviction, endurance, broad understanding and hard work. Thus, this choice should be preceded by thorough analyses and discussions about the problems experienced and the business opportunities. This chapter contains some frequently asked questions and arguments to aid these analyses and discussions.

Why Strive for Lean?

The term Lean has become very popular in recent years in manufacturing operations as well as in other types of operations within different branches. The desire to strive for Lean is often expressed as "we will implement Lean". In this case it is important to answer the enthusiasm by questioning *why*. Striving for Lean only because "all other companies seem to be doing it" is not likely to bring lasting improvements to the operations.

Another reason to be skeptical of statements like "we will implement Lean" is that it signals that the person making the statement has not really understood what Lean is about. Lean is not a method that can be implemented in a few months and then considered to be fully in place. Instead it is a way of relating to operations, a way that prescribes untiring striving to eliminate waste in all its various shapes and forms. Thus, it is an open-ended effort. The operation that is totally free of waste does not exist and will never exist!

For a Lean effort to be meaningful there has to be a real, and accepted, connection to the company's competitiveness. Examples of driving forces are:

- Improved quality
- Reduced costs
- Increased flexibility
- Increased delivery reliability
- Shorter delivery times
- Shorter queue times

In addition to these types of benefits there are others that have more to do with strengthening the workforce's well-being, driving force, motivation and influence. Some examples are:

- Reduced stress
- Increased competence
- Improved co-operation
- Reduced frustration
- Improved customer communication
- Holistic understanding
- Wider and more developing tasks
- Improved safety at the workplace
- Increased job security

These are only a few examples of the positive effects that a Lean effort can bring to an organization. Choosing suppliers that are successful in their Lean effort will bring further benefits, as these suppliers are normally more predictable in their deliveries, which is an important condition for the customer to be able to rationalize his internal flows.

Is it Possible to Succeed without External Support?

There is no general answer to the question of whether it is possible to succeed without external support. Success is dependent on a driving force, commitment and knowledge. Many organizations have come a long way without any deeper knowledge of Lean, and the reason they have succeeded is due to their successful focus on the right things.

A forceful and committed management is necessary for success, regardless of whether they possess Lean knowledge or not. When the operation is small and does not contain overly complex flows, the conditions to succeed without external support are even better.

Unfortunately, it is often the case that both the driving force and the knowledge are missing. However, when at least the will to go for Lean exists it is a good idea to look for external support that can provide the knowledge necessary to get started with the improvement work.

For the external support to bring the desired effect, it is important to dare to try new ways of thinking. Every proposal should of course be carefully considered, but if suggestions are rejected only because results are uncertain it is not possible to succeed. The one who continues doing as he or she has always done will get the same results as usual.

In addition to the transfer of knowledge, external support also plays an important role by suggesting well-functioning ways to apply the Lean principles under the prevailing conditions. Valuable contributions are also to suggest an appropriate improvement work set-up, and a reasonable speed of change. Starting a large number of improvement activities at once is rarely successful.

Undoubtedly there are advantages in using external support, but the improvement work should never be owned by anyone outside the own organization. Management and workforce should understand and implement the improvements hand-in-hand to ensure a continuous, lasting and enduring progress towards Lean.

How Long will it Take?

It certainly is time consuming to fundamentally adopt Lean as a way of relating to operations. How long it will take depends not only on the driving force and the will to change, but also on what the current situation looks like and how mature the organization is in handling changes. Some results may appear already after a few weeks, but the time it takes to have Lean established as a way of thinking in the organization is rather measured in years. The size of the organization is also an important factor. Lean is a way to relate to operations and the more people there are that have to change their mindsets the longer it takes.

Eliminating *all* waste from an operation is impossible so in that sense you will never be finished. Toyota has untiringly reduced waste since the 1950s and they are still not finished. This is a good example showing that Lean is not a project that has an end.

Is Lean Applicable also at Small Volumes?

There are a lot of misunderstandings about Lean, probably because it is the automotive industry that has been leading the development of Lean. Many people believe that the automotive industry's application of Lean is a template for how Lean should be applied. As the automotive industry has conditions different to many other types of operations, a common conclusion is that Lean is not applicable to these other operations. A widespread misunderstanding is that:

> **"Lean will not work in our operations since we have unique products and small volumes"**

There is no connection between Lean on one hand and volumes and product complexity on the other. This statement is supported by the fact that Lean works superbly in e.g. administrative flows. In administrative flows, low volumes as well as complex and abstract products are common. Applying Lean is of course easier when conditions are characterized by a single product and a demand rate that does not vary over time. These were the conditions under which Henry Ford produced the model T. On the other hand, it can be said that the worse the conditions the greater the potential to actually achieve substantial improvements with Lean.

In the beginning Toyota produced small volumes, and TPS was developed to be profitable at these small volumes. Although Toyota's volumes have increased considerably and their yearly production is now very large, they continue producing in small batch sizes. Thus, the success of a Lean effort is determined by how Lean thinking is applied rather than by prevailing conditions.

Usually, volumes are not really as small as it may seem when product variants are studied separately. What matters from a production perspective is how the various products flow through the processes. All products and variants that pass through the same processes can be viewed as belonging to the same product family. The number of product families is normally considerably smaller than the number of products, implying that the volume per product family is larger. When the product families have been identified, focus can be shifted to improving the flow of each product family.

Can Lean be Applied in any Operation?

Lean is still mostly applied in manufacturing operations. There are probably many reasons for this, one important reason being that the first well-known examples and results came from Toyota's motor vehicle manufacturing. Motor vehicle manufacturing is not only assembly, but it comprises a number of different types of manufacturing processes. Therefore it was natural that manufacturers of various kinds realized the possibility of following Toyota's example. Today these manufacturers have worked with Lean for many years with many improvements as a result.

Another reason why Lean continues to be mainly applied in manufacturing is that here flows are often considered easier to improve than non-manufacturing flows. This view probably depends on the possibility of being able to actually see the product and to physically follow the product flow, which makes the improvement work less abstract. In many cases, but far from all, it is true that there is less complexity in manufacturing operations.

In non-manufacturing operations it has previously been widely believed that Lean is not applicable at all. A statement from healthcare illustrates this:

"We do not produce products, we work with people"

However, in recent years the work of applying Lean as a way to relate to operations has increased significantly within non-manufacturing operations, and the results speak for themselves. Many larger organizations in healthcare, banking, services, etc. have achieved such significant results that they have even created their own departments working full time to support the rest of the organization in their Lean efforts. In addition, many manufacturing companies that previously had applied Lean only in manufacturing have now taken their Lean effort further to product development, administration, etc.

The most typical problems regarding efficiency within non-manufacturing operations stem from flow problems, and this is exactly where Lean has its greatest impact. Lean is not primarily about performing surgical operations faster, changing the content of a car service, etc. Instead, focus is put on all those things that happen between the value-adding parts of a flow. Therefore all kinds of operations can benefit from working with Lean.

A necessary requirement to be successful with Lean is to be able to see the abstract products that are produced in non-manufacturing operations. When it is clear to the members of the workforce that the produced products in e.g. an accounts department are various kinds of basic financial data, it will be easier for them to start picturing the flows and their own role in them. Having achieved this understanding creates the right conditions for starting an effective improvement work.

Why do not More Organizations Fully Adopt Lean?

Considering all the benefits it brings it is natural to question why more organizations have not fully adopted Lean. There has been a considerable increase in organizations that have adopted Lean during the last few years, but still all too many run their operations in a more traditional way.

A possible reason for this is that Lean is a way of relating to operations that requires a lot of work, work that does not always yield quick results. Another reason may be that some organizations have misunderstood Lean, for example organizations which equate Lean with motor vehicle manufacturing. There may, moreover, be misgivings about the role changes that come with a Lean effort. The influence of the workforce is greatly increased and each manager gets an important role as a teacher and coach, and this division of roles may be distasteful to some people. Other common objections to Lean are:

- There is no excess time, which means that everyone has to produce
- The workforce lacks the will to change due to numerous (failed) attempts at performing "similar" improvement efforts previously
- The company is doing well and therefore there is no reason to improve the operations
- There is no one within the company who wants to, or has the energy to, drive the work
- There is an unwillingness or a fear of giving responsibility and authority to the workforce
- It takes a very long time so it might as well be done later
- The company cannot afford to fail

Some of these objections are probably familiar. The way to avoid them is to increase understanding and to mobilize the courage to dare to try.

Are there no Drawbacks with Lean?

In the literature Lean is sometimes described in almost religious terms. It is easy to get the impression that a Lean effort is the solution to all problems and, in addition, that it is a solution that always works. This is of course not the case. On the other hand, the negative articles that are published now and then do not present the absolute truth either.

It is perfectly clear that Lean can be both good and bad just like anything else. Whether or not a Lean effort will bring the desired results and also be appreciated by the workforce depends entirely on how it is carried out. This is not different from any other effort to change an operation. Two pitfalls that should be avoided above all are:

- The operations are challenged too much
- Efficiency gains are handled in the wrong way

It was made clear early in this book that resource-efficient is a better description of Lean than resource-meagre. This means that an operation is at its most efficient when it has the right resources, not when it has as few resources as possible. If the operation is challenged in such a way that it is experienced as being stressful, and that it suffers from too many disturbances, etc., the Lean effort will not succeed. The result will be that the workforce as well as the customers will suffer, and this of course is not the intention with Lean. This kind of unsound application will give Lean a bad reputation.

Another pitfall is that the achieved benefits from an improved way of working are instantly exploited by e.g. reducing personnel. Acting in that manner will kill any ambition to improve. How is it possible to motivate people to find ways to improve the operation when the consequence is that the personnel will suffer?

Thus, for the Lean effort to be successful in the long term, it is extremely important that the achieved productivity gains are handled in the correct way. In successful cases, the freed resources are, in the short term, used to expand the improvement work. In the longer term it may instead be wise to utilize the freed capacity to take on new orders. However, it is important not to use all the freed capacity for this. To be able to maintain the speed of the improvement work, the workforce should be allowed to use a certain amount of time every week to work on improvements.

Thoughts on the Way towards Lean

Finally some words on the way towards Lean, intended for those who have already started their endless journey towards Lean as well as those who are facing the decision whether to take it on or not. Perhaps the most important insight is that an operation will be no more successful than the organization's understanding of Lean permits it to be. When Lean principles are applied in the correct way they provide excellent conditions for creating a competitive and profitable operation. The challenge is to be able to create practical ways of applying the Lean principles so that they will produce the desired effects under the prevailing conditions. Lean requires a holistic perspective, and at the same time an understanding that actual improvements can only be accomplished through attention to details.

Another important insight is that Lean is a way of relating to operations. Changing an entire organization's way of relating to operations is a change of mindset that takes time and requires that management is convinced and persistent. Basically, it is viewing the operations in another way and actually *wanting* to detect waste. The goal is to make the entire organization understand that the detected waste, i.e. the deviations, is something positive in the sense that it reveals possibilities of improving the operation. Such an attitude to the operation provides the right conditions for turning the deviations into success!

Standards are beneficial in most cases but standardized problem solving, in the form of tackling all problems with the same method, is counter-productive.

Ap

Appendix: A Small Selection of Lean Methods

This appendix presents overall descriptions of a few Lean methods. It is only a small selection and countless texts have been written on most of them. The bibliography presents some of the more detailed descriptions of these methods.

The Lean principles together with the problems at hand should be the starting point when choosing a method. When conditions differ, it is natural that different methods should be used to solve the same type of problem in different parts of the value stream. Thus, the choice of method should be preceded by a thorough analysis. However, it happens all too often that a method is chosen more or less randomly in the belief that all Lean methods will always yield improvements. A method that has been described earlier in this book is Kanban, which is used to order materials and production. This method requires certain conditions in order to deliver the desired effect.

Figure A - 1. *The choice of method should be preceded by a thorough analysis in order to bring the desired effect. A random choice of method is likely to result in failure.*

The fact that some methods have been successful in one flow does not mean that they will be so in the next. Standards are beneficial in most cases but standardized problem solving, in the form of tackling all problems with the same method, is counter-productive.

Five common methods that are typical examples of Lean methods will be described in this appendix. These are not methods that should always have top priority in the improvement work, but the methods all have their specific aims and some of them are intended to be used at the flow level while others belong to the process level of a value stream.

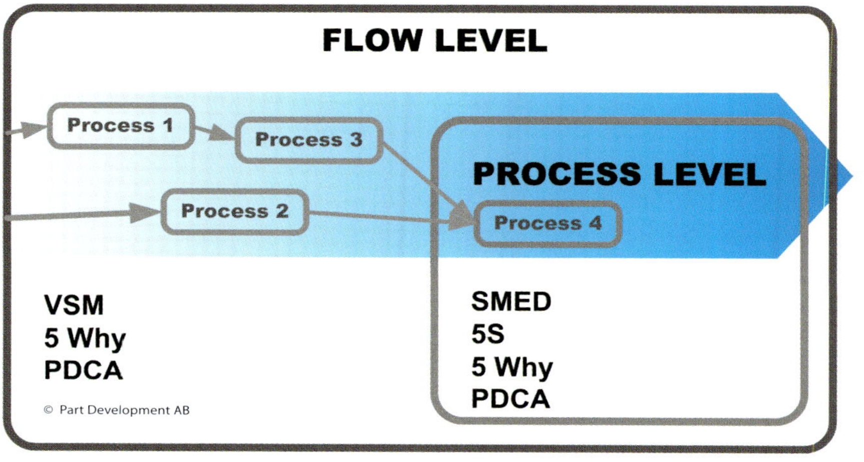

Figure A - 2. *The described methods' applicability at different levels of a value stream.*

Value Stream Mapping

A value stream comprises all the steps, both value-adding and not, from picking raw materials to delivery to the customer. The primary aim of the method Value Stream Mapping is to widen the perspective from a narrow focus on single processes to an overview of the entire production system. Focus is put on the efficiency of the *flow* rather than on the efficiency of individual units and processes. Value Stream Mapping is applied at the following levels of an operation:

- Flow level (end-to-end internal flow)
- Supply chain level (supplier-factory-customer)

Before the method Value Stream Mapping is applied, that which will add customer value should be known. In addition, the product families should have been identified. This is described in Chapter 6. Given this information Value Stream Mapping is carried out in two steps. The first step is to create a map of the current value stream (current state), and the second is to make an analysis based on the current state and the Lean principles. Based on this analysis a new map is drawn that describes a desired future value stream (future state). The description of the desired future value stream constitutes the basis for the creation of an action plan on how the practical work to change the value stream should be carried out.

Mapping the Current State

Finding out how the operation works in detail is a crucial first step. If changes are made without having a common, correct view of how the operation works at present, there is considerable risk that the wrong actions to modify the operation will be taken.

Most often the method Value Stream Mapping is applied at the flow level within e.g. a factory. The value stream is mapped from the incoming materials to shipping. Within a factory there are normally many different value streams, and to be able to perform the mapping with a reasonable work effort a specific flow such as a product family is often chosen. When the method is used for the first time it would be advisable to choose a relatively simple value stream.

The mapping should be carried out by a group of people that together have proper knowledge of the entire value stream. The first step of the mapping is to walk along the flow, preferably upstream, and identify all the process steps that the chosen part passes through. The group draws this sequence of process steps on paper.

In flows where the product is not physically observable, such as in administrative flows, the method Value Stream Mapping may appear difficult to apply. Mapping in this kind of value streams will not be successful without a good understanding of the meaning of the various flow terms. One example is to view the inbox in the computer's email program as a point of storage (buffer).

After mapping the process, the group returns to the flow in order to map the part's way through the flow. This time they make an inventory of all buffers and storage spaces before and after each process step. At every process step information is collected about those properties that are considered relevant. Some examples are:

- Cycle time
- Process time
- Possible change-over time
- Batch sizes
- Number of variants
- Availability
- Actual capacity
- Scrap rate
- Number of operators
- Shift form/Work hours
- Delivery volume
- Production control

As a first step the information available is collected, but more information may possibly be needed at a later stage. The collected information is noted under each process on the hand-drawn map. The map is complemented with information about the customer and the supplier. How the material arrives at the factory and how the part is delivered to the customer is also included in the map, e.g. by truck symbols. Information about frequency and quantity is added to the transport symbols.

Under each process on the map the time it takes for the part to pass through that process is noted. This time is called the value-adding time in the method Value Stream Mapping.

Next to the symbol for each buffer/storage, the time (based on the customer demand rate) it will take until the buffer/storage is empty (storage time) is noted. When the customer demands e.g. 78 parts per day and the buffer contains 171 parts, it means that 2.2 days is noted on the map.

The sum of the storage times for all buffers and storages, together with the sum of all process times constitutes the lead time. This lead time is compared to the total value-adding time. It is not unusual that the total value-adding time is measured in parts per mille, rather than in parts per cent, of the total lead time.

When all facts about the processes and intermediate storages have been entered, the map is completed with information on how often and in what way orders are made by customers, and sent to suppliers, as well as how the various processes are controlled. This information might be extracted from weekly schedules of the company's MPC system, control levels in buffers, etc.

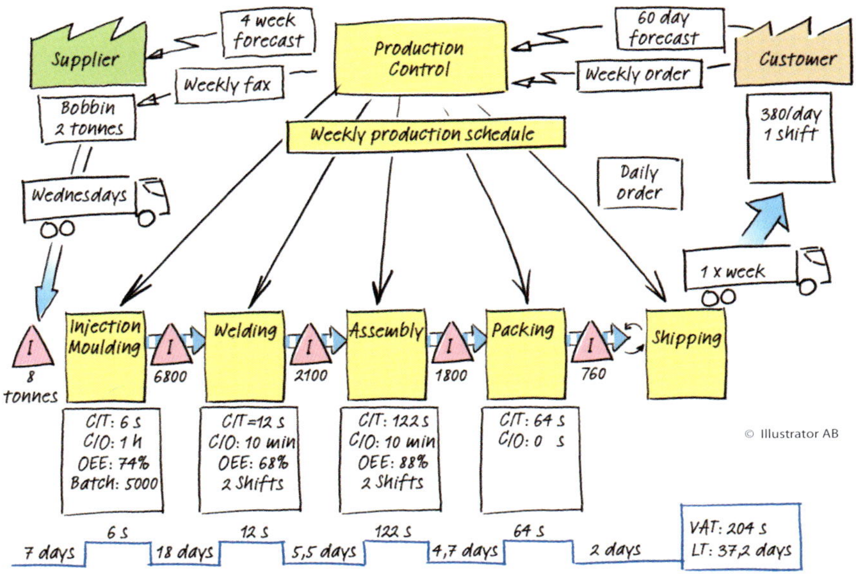

Figure A - 3. *Example of a map of the current state after the first step of the method Value Stream Mapping.*

An important characteristic of the method Value Stream Mapping is that it comprises an analysis not only of the product and material flows, but also of the information flow. To achieve a good result it is necessary to know how production is controlled and how information is exchanged within the company. In most cases the information flow is very complex, often considerably more so than necessary.

Future State

It is sometimes tempting to immediately proceed with improvement work after completing the mapping of the current situation. However, this leads to unnecessary risks, as a value stream is complex in nature and as it sometimes contains dependencies that make outcomes difficult to predict. The second step of the method Value Stream Mapping is to create a map of a desired future state in order to provide an unambiguous and agreed picture of the goal of the improvement work. This is equally important as having a blueprint when building a house.

Creating a map of the desired future state based on the mapping of the present situation is accomplished by applying the Lean principles. Reduced lead times is a common goal in Value Stream Mapping and this normally requires that the process steps in the value stream should be linked tighter to each other. In this way the products, whether physical or not, can flow more efficiently through the processes. This is one example of how the principle Continuous flow may be applied.

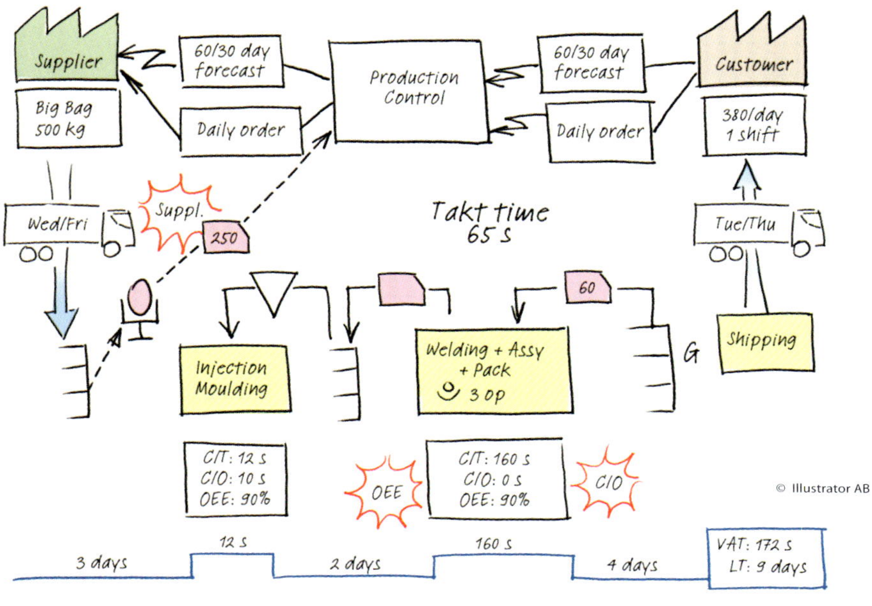

Figure A - 4. *Example of a map over the desired future state derived from the second step of the method Value Stream Mapping.*

In some non-manufacturing operations there may be a need for other kinds of visualization models than the one presented above. One alternative that may be suitable in these cases is called the Swimlane model. Swimlane is an alternative way of presenting the results from the method Value Stream Mapping. An advantage of the Swimlane model is that interactions between different departments/occupations are made clear.

The mapping starts by identifying the departments/occupations of interest for the studied flow. Each department/occupation is represented by a swimlane. All activities that take place in the flow are then mapped into the respective swimlane in the right sequence. Information and documentation that are relevant to the task are attached to the activities. The intended documentation may e.g. be the result of an activity that is printed and posted together with the activity. One example of such a result is basic tender data. Visualizing results in this way clarifies what is happening in the flow. It also shows to what point the documentation is refined at different stages along the flow.

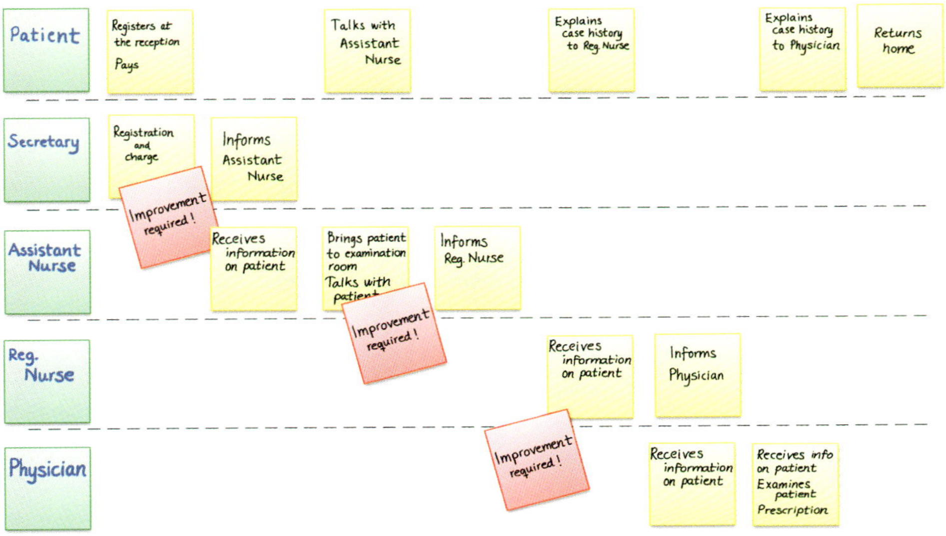

Figure A-5. *An example of a Swimlane map, describing the current state of a flow of patients.*

Based on the map of the current state and suggested improvements, a map over the desired future state is created.

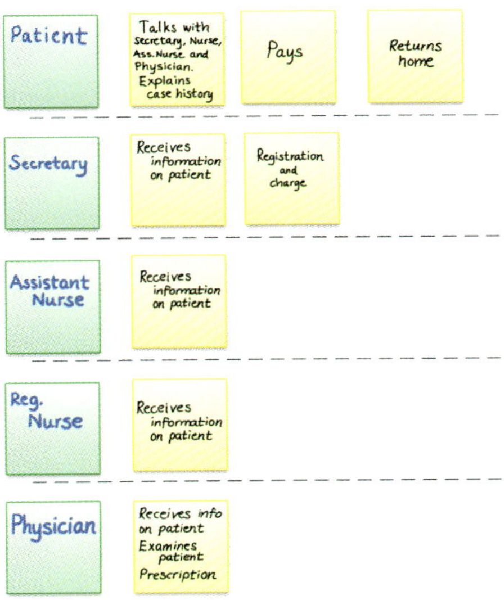

Figure A-6. *An example of a Swimlane map, describing the desired future state of a flow of patients.*

In Chapter 5 various forms of waste were presented. Two of them are transport and motion. These forms of waste include the transport of materials and products as well as the movement of people. In applying the method Value Stream Mapping this waste can be visualized by using a Spaghetti chart.

The process of creating a Spaghetti chart starts with a layout of the operation. The next step is to follow the physical movements of the product/customer/patient and to draw a line for every movement. The result is normally a large number of long lines. The method has got its name from the fact that the long lines often look like cooked spaghetti.

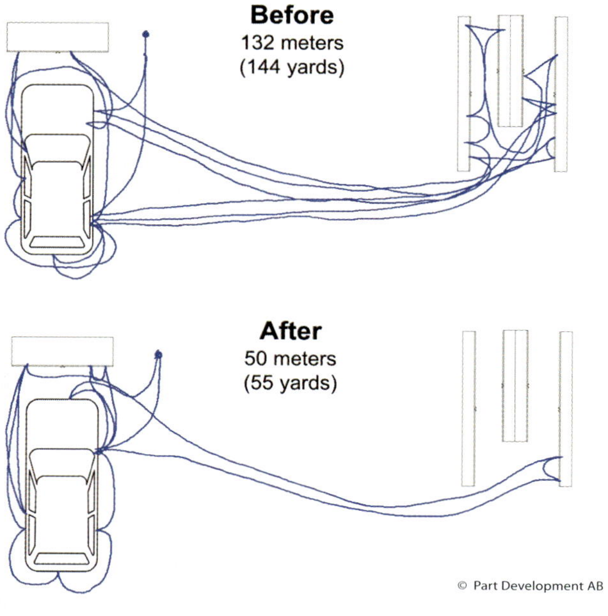

Figure A-7. *Example of a Spaghetti chart from a car servicing workshop, before and after improved ways of working.*

The equivalent of transport waste can also be found in e.g. administrative flows. It might be the need to switch between various information systems to fetch or feed information. It may also be how an order or a case passes through various departments or functions of an operation. To visualize this kind of waste the Spaghetti chart variant shown in Figure A-8 may be applied.

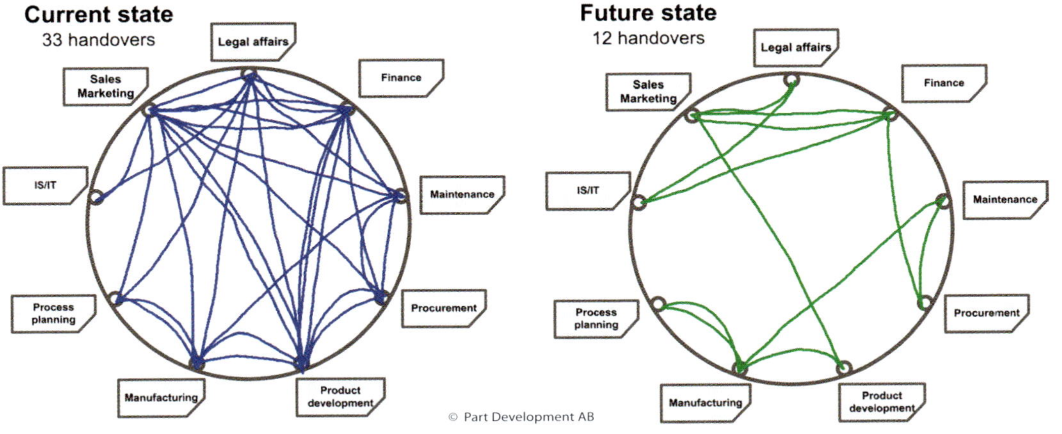

Figure A-8. *Example of a Spaghetti chart from an administrative flow where a case passes through a number of departments, before and after improved ways of working.*

Tips and Experiences

Today, the method Value Stream Mapping is widely spread and is for example described in the book "Learning to See" (Rother and Shook, 1998). However, as with so many other things there is scope for interpretation. Some common problems together with brief descriptions on how they can be solved are presented below.

Mapping is the Goal

Mapping the present situation may lead to an improved understanding of the flows at hand, but it does not necessarily lead to measurable improvements. After all, mapping does not solve any problems by itself. What determines whether the operation will improve or not are the activities performed in order to improve the value stream.

Perfect Map of the Current State

For those individuals who have been working for many years on improvements at the process level, it may be easy to get stuck in overly detailed analyses. The details together make the whole and are naturally important, but to perform a Value Steam Mapping with reasonable effort it may still be effective to think "better to be almost right than exactly wrong". It should also be mentioned that there are information overlaps and feedback loops between the steps in the current state and the future state.

Group Composition

The method Value Stream Mapping aims to improve a flow from door to door. It is normally applied over organizational borders, and therefore the work to improve the flow should be led by someone who has the authority to shape the *entire* value stream: a task like that should not be delegated. Further, the group performing the Value Stream Mapping should be composed of people representing a cross section of the roles present in the flow. This means that planning personnel, operators, technicians, supervisors, etc. should all be included. There is normally also a need to include representatives from other functions such as purchasing and marketing as they, to a large extent, affect the conditions of the flow.

The Future is Far Away

When describing the future state it is common to set the "optimal solution" as the goal. This is likely to lead to a situation where taking the first step from the current situation is felt to be too difficult. The vision of the "optimal solution" is important so that everyone can see where the operation is heading, but from a practical improvement perspective the next future state should be no more than 6-12 months away. With this time scale it is much clearer which improvements are reasonable and suitable just then. In addition, it becomes possible for the organization to handle the action plan.

Although it is relatively simple, Value Stream Mapping is a powerful method. However, when it is applied in the wrong way it may be counter-productive. In addition to the problems stated above there is the risk that wrong ways of working will be reinforced during the design of the future state. To avoid this, it is important that there is a proper understanding of Lean within the group.

One of the major aims in performing Value Stream Mapping is to create a *common* view of the flow. Many people think that it is unnecessary to walk around the flow and sketch with pen and paper. However, the point of doing this is that every participant sees the same things, i.e. they see how things work and not how things are intended to work. The viewing, sketching, erasing and re-sketching entail a lot of manual work, but it is nonetheless an important learning cycle. It is the creation of the map rather than the map itself that teaches the organization to see.

SMED – A Method to Reduce Change-over Times

Change-over time is usually defined as the time between the completion of one batch and the first approved part in the next batch. From a flow perspective, change-over times should be as short as possible in order to provide beneficial conditions to produce in small batch sizes. Another example of change-over time is the time elapsed from the point where one patient is fully stitched up in one operating room until the knife is put into the next patient in the same operating room.

A common method for change-over time reduction is SMED. This is an acronym for “Single-digit Minute Exchange of Die”, i.e. changing dies in less than ten minutes. The SMED method is based on the fact that change-over time can be divided into two parts:

- Internal change-over time
- External change-over time

Internal change-over time is the time for the change-over work that requires that the equipment is not running. External change-over time, on the other hand, is the time spent on the change-over between products while the equipment is running.

At an overall level SMED concerns:

- Separating internal and external change-over times
- Transforming internal change-over time to external change-over time
- Rationalizing all elements in the change-over

SMED is applicable to most change-over processes even if the method in the beginning was developed for changing dies in presses. The method contains eight techniques, some not always applicable:

1. Separate Internal and External Change-over Times
   This fundamental rule is to separate what can be performed while the equipment is still running from that which cannot. An example of the former is the picking of new tools.

2. Transform Internal Change-over Time to External Change-over Time
   In unbiased reviews of the change-over process it has been shown that in most cases surprisingly many tasks can actually be performed while the equipment is still running. For example: In most cases the loading and adjusting of tools and fixtures can be done before they are installed into the equipment.

3. Functional Standardization

It would be easy if all tools and add-ons pertaining to a machine had the same shape and dimensions. Most often it is more profitable to standardize only certain attachment points of the tools and let the other shapes and measures be free to be set for exactly that tool. A particular procedure for a particular function can often be used for the entire machine. An example is the fastening of tools.

4. Functional Fastening Devices

Screws are the most common fasteners for attaching a tool to a machine. However, screws are rarely the simplest or fastest fasteners. Time can be saved by not having to rotate a tool more turns than necessary to achieve fastening. Time can also be saved by replacing bolted joints by e.g. clamping devices. When bolted joints cannot be replaced, it is advantageous that they have the same size so that the same hand tools can be used.

5. Pre-adjusted Fixtures

In some cases the change-over time can be reduced by the use of fixtures to which the work piece can be fastened. In this manner the next blank can be clamped into a fixture while the equipment is still running. The entire fixture with the work piece is installed in the equipment and the change of the work piece can be made in the available fixture. This procedure requires that the position of the fixtures in the equipment is set so that adjustments can be made between the fixture and the work piece.

6. Perform Work Tasks in Parallel

It is often the case that change-overs are performed by only one person. In this case a lot of time is spent by the operator moving between e.g. the front and the back of the equipment. By dividing the work between two people, working on different sides of the equipment, much time can be saved.

7. Eliminate Adjustments

Adjustments are common during change-overs and this work is time consuming. By the use of locating pins, jigs, etc., tools and limiting switches can be fitted into the correct positions at once. This may eliminate the need for adjustments.

8. Mechanizing

The attachment of tools and fixtures can sometimes be mechanized.

The first step in the SMED analysis is to document a normal change-over and clock each work element. After that, the group analyzing the change-over (preferably the users of the equipment) classifies each element. That is, they determine whether it is required that the equipment is not running (internal change-over) or if it is possible to execute the work element while the equipment is still running (external change-over). The analysis is facilitated by filming the work, as it enables the group to watch various sequences and to have discussions based on facts. After the analysis, the group suggests a new method for performing the change-over of the equipment and they also test this new method.

As for all work procedures, it is important to be well-prepared and to have orderliness at the workplace during a change-over. The method of carrying out a change-over should also be standardized in the same manner as any other work. An improved method to perform faster change-overs has little value if it is not consistently adopted by everyone.

A change-over process can be compared to a change of wheels during a Formula 1 race. In the pit there are a lot of people who are equipped with advanced and expensive tools, but you never see anyone looking for tools. Similarly, you never see anyone who has just taken off a wheel walking away to look for the new one. A change-over at a factory is rarely this well organized.

Figure A - 9. *Well-organized and focused wheel exchange at a Formula 1 pit-stop.*

5 S – Well-organized and Functional Workplace

The method 5 S is often a natural starting point for an organization's Lean effort. The reason is that the method is considered easy to understand and, moreover, orderliness is an important result of the method. To many people 5 S and orderliness are equated, while orderliness in itself is all too often associated with various cleaning activities. This conception does not do justice to 5 S. The method 5 S actually concerns creating a well-organized and functional workplace with the right attitudes and behavior. A well-organized and functional workplace is a basic requirement for being able to standardize the work at the workplace. This is in turn a requirement for eliminating waste.

Figure A - 10. *A well-organized and functional workplace is a basic requirement for the standardization of work.*

A well-organized and functional workplace provides great opportunities for improving productivity. In many companies a large portion of the work hours is spent looking for tools, materials and information. In some cases it is as much as 25 per cent of the work time, i.e. 10 hours per week per person. Thus, working with 5 S can bring about a significant capacity increase with minimal or no investments. It is therefore natural that many companies apply, or try to apply, 5 S. However, all too often the effort fails and the question then is of course *why*.

One reason for failure is that the effort has been underestimated. As mentioned previously, it is not enough to only create orderliness; the attitude and behavior of the workforce must also be changed. The goal is to create an atmosphere where common standards are applied and where the members of the workforce continuously strive to improve the operation in order to reduce waste. Such a change of mindset takes time.

To be successful with the method it is necessary for management to explain *why* 5 S is important. In order to motivate the workforce to take the first steps – hard and unglamorous steps – towards orderliness, it is necessary to instill in them an understanding of the effects of a well-organized and functional workplace on the company's competitiveness. There are of course many ways to spread this understanding. Apart from logical discussions about the relationships between the workplace and company performance, it is usually wise to continuously follow up important performance indicators which will show that the effort actually brings results.

Five Elements

The method 5 S is aimed at eliminating waste through the creation of a well-organized and functional workplace, where everyone knows where the objects are placed and what they are used for. Having the right object in the right place and everything ready to be used is essential within 5 S. The method comprises five different elements, each one of them beginning with the letter S.

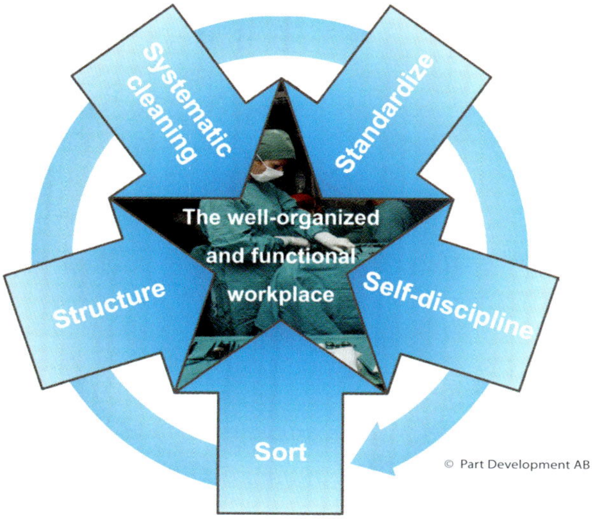

Figure A-11. *The five elements of 5S.*

1. Seiri – Sort

In order to achieve clearness at the workplace, the first step is to sort the objects (tools, materials, etc.) within the work area. The goal is to separate objects that are frequently used from objects that are rarely or never used. Objects that are frequently used should be placed where they are used, and the objects that are not used should be removed from the area as soon as possible.

2. Seiton – Structure

Each object used should have its own specific place. Tools that are used for e.g. a change-over should of course be placed where the change-over takes place. Documents should be filed in a way that people will not have to spend time looking for them, which requires a well-organized file structure and a standardized way of naming documents. Being able to easily detect if an object is missing, i.e. a deviation, is as important as being aware of where it should be placed.

3. Seiso – Systematic Cleaning

Systematic cleaning is not so much about cleaning as about making sure that everything is in order and works as intended. This is similar to the difference between cleaning a car and inspecting it. An efficient set-up implies that the cleaning phase is short and that more time is spent ensuring that everything is in good condition. It is moreover important to take actions to eliminate the root cause of the need for cleaning.

Figure A - 12. *Systematic cleaning is ensuring that everything is in order and that it works as intended. It is not cleanliness in itself that is the point.*

4. Seiketsu – Standardize

When the first three steps have been carried out and the team is in agreement on how things should work, it is time to standardize the way of working. The standardization can be viewed as a handshake or an agreement that the new set-up that the members of the workforce have created in the work area is valid. The standard may e.g. state which objects should be placed at each workplace, what the various cleaning routines should be, how new tools should be ordered, how the various objects should be structured, etc. It is important to create simple standards that are easy to understand and apply. A set-up that requires a lot of administration and is difficult to update will moreover be difficult to maintain in the long run.

5. Shitsuke – Self-discipline

Making the workforce apply the agreed standards is often the most difficult, but also the most important element. The reason is that, to a major extent, it requires changing attitudes and behavior. In some cases it may take several years to reach success with this way of working, as it is based on the workforce's own search for improvements. Therefore, it is important that management understands that it takes time to change attitudes and behavior, otherwise there is a risk that their commitment will slowly disappear. When management stops expecting a certain way of working, whatever it may be, it will soon be abandoned by the workforce.

Success Factors in 5 S

A clear presentation of the problem and a committed management that succeeds in involving the workforce are required to succeed with 5 S. Applying the method solely to bring orderliness most often results in a kind of cleaning project which will not be successful in the long run.

In addition, it is not enough for management to start the work by appointing a person as responsible for the effort and by training the workforce. To achieve lasting improvements it is crucial that management also continuously demands results in a suitable manner, and that they let the employees, on the job, inform them about their recent improvements and what the next step will be. In the same way as the method 5 S is often a suitable first step for the workforce, it is normally also a good opportunity for the managers to start practicing Lean leadership from the ground up.

In addition to the creation of a well-organized and functional workplace, the workforce needs to learn how to run an effective improvement work effort. As the beginning of the 5S effort often entails relatively simple measures, it may be suitable to start training the workforce already from the beginning in systematic problem solving, so that they will gradually be able to deal with more and more advanced deviations.

The work to implement a structured way of working takes time because it takes time to increase understanding. Therefore, implementation in small and controlled steps is recommended as this provides the right conditions for everyone to gain understanding. It moreover enables the workforce to ensure that everything works correctly before the next step is taken. When changes are too rapid, there is a risk that the way of working will not be established and that it will soon fade away.

Important from a Holistic Perspective

A well-organized and functional workplace normally generates commitment in the workforce. A well-organized and functional workplace is also a basic condition for being able to standardize manual work and thus achieve predictability at the process level. The standards enable the detection of deviations as what is normal and what is not becomes clearer and clearer. The more deviations that can be resolved, the more predictable the process will be. In this way the 5 S method contributes to making processes more predictable.

Predictable processes in turn provide the right conditions for eliminating waste throughout the entire value stream. This may take the form of reducing buffer sizes, as predictability at process level means that the variations in cycle times, change-over times, etc. are small.

PDCA – Structure of the Improvement Work

Deviations drive improvement work, but how is the improvement work performed? Implementing improvements is the core of Lean, and the improvements have to be continuous otherwise the improvement work will soon die out. The entire operation should be permeated by this improvement work at all levels, through all internal processes and flows all the way out into the external value streams.

The Four Phases

PDCA is an effective method of structuring improvement work. The method is sometimes called the Deming cycle after its originator W. Edwards Deming. The PDCA method gives structure to the improvement work. It is divided into four phases: Plan, Do, Check and Act, and these are performed cyclically one after the other.

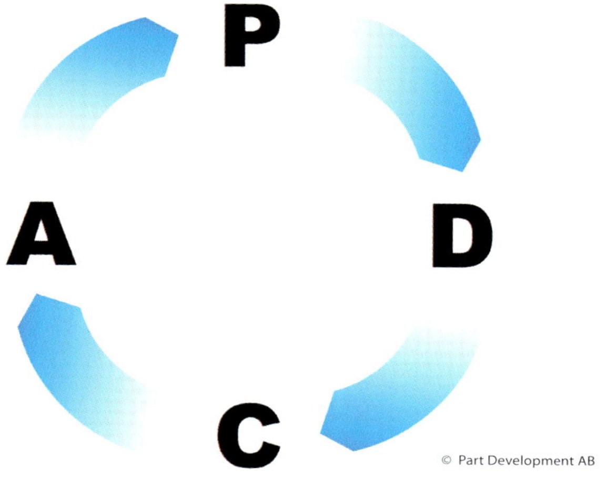

Figure A - 13. *The PDCA cycle with its four phases: Plan, Do, Check and Act.*

Plan

The work in this phase is not only planning what should be done, but it also comprises the work to define the customer's (internal and/or external) needs, to collect data, to identify and analyze the problem, and to identify the root cause of the problem. The root cause is the real cause of a detected problem. The planning phase also comprises goal setting and the creation of a project plan. Communication is an important part of this phase, as all parties involved need continuous information and have to be able to influence the project so that good results are achieved.

Do

When the planning phase has been properly carried out the implementation phase becomes relatively easy. The problem is clearly defined, the root cause is identified and everyone is aware of what should be done. Thus, the Do phase is carrying out the activities stated in the plan.

Check

This phase includes most of the learning, independent of the outcome of the implementation phase. The check phase not only consists of comparing the results with the goals, but moreover other questions need to be answered, such as:

- What was said about the root cause in the planning phase?
- What worked well and what did not work so well?
- What lessons have been learned for the remainder of the work and for the upcoming improvement work?

Act

When the improvement work is successful, the new, improved level should be secured. The improvement has taken the operation from one level to a new and better one. This new level should be secured by a new standard and thus the circle is closed, with the new standard opening the possibility to detect more deviations.

After a completed PDCA cycle, it should be considered whether the standard can be disseminated and applied somewhere else. It is also important to celebrate when the improvement work has been a success; such positive actions have a great influence on the long-term survival of the improvement work. Working with improvements has to contain an element of fun.

Many Application Areas

PDCA as a method constitutes the basis of all improvement work. It is therefore sometimes a necessary ingredient in other methods and overall procedures. There is e.g. a clear connection between the Improvement wheel, described in Chapter 4, and the PDCA cycle. The PDCA cycle describes more detailed procedures in the analysis and improvement parts of the Improvement wheel.

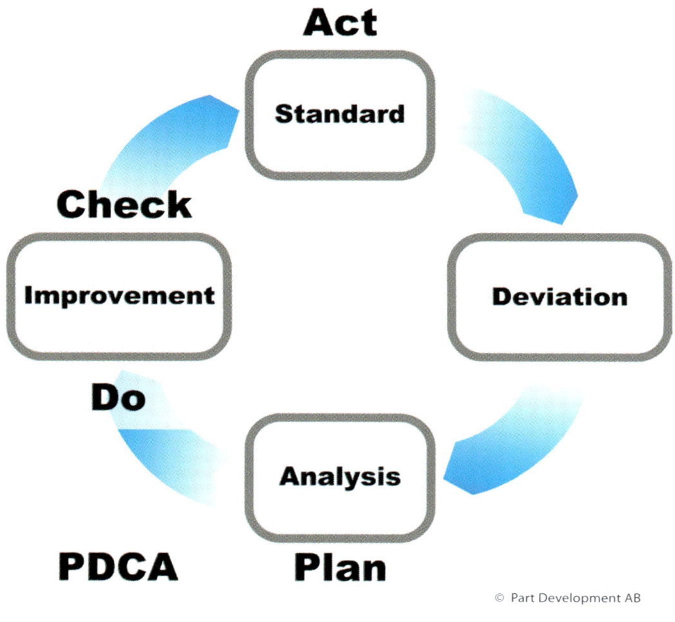

Figure A - 14. *Similarities between the PDCA cycle and the Improvement wheel.*

PDCA is also a useful method in 5S. The aim of 5S is to create a well-organized and functional workplace, but the workforce also needs to learn how to drive an efficient improvement work effort. With PDCA, the workforce can structure their improvement work to be efficient. At the beginning of the 5S effort, the problems dealt with are normally relatively easy to solve, and it may be suitable to train the workforce in how to use the PDCA cycle already at that point in order to gradually become able to cope with increasingly complex problems. The same discussion is valid for other methods such as SMED.

Root Cause Analysis with 5 Why

The work to eliminate waste is central within Lean but unfortunately it is not as easy as it may sound. There are three main difficulties in the work to eliminate waste:

- To detect the waste
- To analyze the waste
- To identify the right measures so that the waste will not recur

To be able to detect waste it is necessary to define what is normal. This will in turn require standardization. With standardization that which is abnormal, i.e. that is waste, will be made evident.

The Method 5 Why

The analysis method 5 Why is, from a theoretical point of view, a very simple method for finding the root cause of a detected deviation, i.e. of a concrete form of waste. That the method is theoretically simple means that it is easy to learn and conceptualize. However, this is not to say that it is easy to use it in the correct way to actually identify the root cause of a deviation.

Applying 5 Why to find the root cause of a detected deviation means asking the question *why* five times. For every answer one penetrates deeper into the problem and gets closer to the real cause of the deviation. The first questions are normally relatively easy to formulate, but for every new question it becomes increasingly difficult.

Figure A - 15. *Every new question is more difficult to formulate than the previous one.*

When the question why has been posed and answered for the fifth time, the root cause of the deviation should have been identified. This is where the actions should be initiated. When it is possible to resolve the root cause so that the deviation will never recur, then the method has succeeded. The example below shows how the method 5 Why works.

Root Cause Analysis with 5 Why ***Example***

One of five screws for a bracket was not tightened to the right torque

1 Why: **Why were not all the five screws tightened to the right torque?**

Answer: *The assembly operator missed tightening the fifth screw.*

2 Why: **Why was tightening of the fifth screw missed?**

Answer: *Because the assembly operator was interrupted by a colleague during assembly.*

3 Why: **Why did this interruption result in that tightening of the screw was missed?**

Answer: *It was not clear to the assembly operator which screws had been tightened.*

4 Why: **Why was it unclear to the assembly operator which screws had been tightened?**

Answer: *All screws had been placed and screwed to the bottom by hand so that they appeared to be tightened.*

5 Why: **Why were all screws screwed to the bottom so that they appeared to be tightened?**

Answer: *According to the standardized work, all screws should be screwed to the bottom by hand before they are tightened.*

Root cause: A problem in the standardized work.

Possible measure to take so that the problem will never recur:

Modify the standardized work so that every screw is tightened directly after being placed. In this way it will be visible to the eye which screws have been tightened.

Success Factors with 5 Why

To succeed in identifying the root cause using 5 Why, it is important that the deviation to be solved is specific. It is not possible to solve general problems using this method. An example of a problem that is far too general is why a process on the average has 65 minutes of stop time per shift. There are probably a great number of different reasons for this. Every stop that has occurred has its own history and thus its own root cause.

Thus, for the method 5 Why to be useful each specific deviation has to be identified and handled separately. In the stop time example above, *one* specific stop would have been chosen and analyzed to ascertain why *that* specific stop occurred. The fact that there are perhaps 100 other possible causes to a similar stop does not matter. With 5 Why one deviation at a time is analyzed.

The method 5 Why questions the *process,* never a person. This requires that management has the mindset that all members of the workforce are doing their best at work. When things still go wrong, it is the conditions, i.e. the process, that should be questioned. This is a way of promoting a positive work atmosphere where the employees actually want to highlight the deviations they detect.

When a person has e.g. failed in a manual assembly process, it is pointless to blame the person and ask why he or she failed. This usually ends up with the person promising never to repeat the mistake again. Who can guarantee that? If this person did his/her best, the problem may very well occur the next time the same person does his/her best unless the conditions for getting it right have been improved.

Thus, it is the process that should be questioned, and in practice this means that it is the person's conditions that are questioned. The real problem may be training, aids, standardized work, etc.

Bibliography

Bicheno, J. (2004),
The New Lean Toolbox: Towards Fast, Flexible Flow,
PICSIE Books, Buckingham, U.K.,
ISBN 978-0954124410

Bicheno, J. (2008),
The Lean Toolbox for Service Systems,
PICSIE Books, Buckingham, U.K.,
ISBN 978-0-9541244-4-1

Cochran, D.S. (1998),
Introduction to Production System Design: The System Design Differences Between Mass and Lean Production,
MIT-Visteon Lean Manufacturing Workshop,
September 2-4, Monroe MI, USA

George, M.L. (2006),
Lean Six Sigma for Services,
McGraw Hill, Seoul, Korea,
ISBN 89-88825-87-X.

Johnson, T., Bröms, A. (2000),
Profit Beyond Measure,
The Free Press, New York, USA,
ISBN 0-684-83667-X

Maskell, B., Baggaley, B. (2003),
Practical Lean Accounting – A Proven System for Measuring and Managing the Lean Enterprise,
Productivity Press, New York, USA,
ISBN 9781563272431

Ohno, T. (1988),
Toyota Production System – Beyond Large-Scale Production,
Productivity Press, New York, USA
ISBN 978-0-915299-14-0

Petersson, P. (2000),
Process Efficiency and Capacity Flexibility, Doctoral thesis,
Dept. of Mechanical Engineering, LiU, Linkoping, Sweden,
ISBN 91-7219-656-4

Rother, M., Shook, J. (1998),
Learning to See – Value Stream Mapping to Add Value and Eliminate Muda,
Lean Enterprise Institute, Inc., MA, USA,
ISBN 0-974-3225-7-1

Sandkull, B., Johansson, J. (2000),
Från Taylor till Toyota,
Studentlitteratur, Lund, Sweden,
ISBN 91-44-01346-9

Seddon, J. (2005),
Freedom from Command & Control,
Vanguard Press, Buckingham, U.K.,
ISBN 978-0-9546183-0-8

Shingo, S. (1985),
Revolution in Manufacturing: The SMED System,
Productivity Press, New York, USA,
ISBN 978-0-915299-03-4

Shingo, S. (1989),
Study of Toyota Production System,
Productivity Press, New York, USA,
ISBN 978-0-915299-17-1

Spear, S.J. (2004),
Learning to Lead at Toyota,
Harvard Business Review, Length: 12p,
Publication Date: May, 2004

Spear, S.J., Bowen, H.K. (1999),
Decoding the DNA of the Toyota Production System,
Harvard Business Review, Length: 13p,
Publication Date: September, 1999

Womack, P.J. (2003),
Move Your Operations to China? Do some Lean math first,
Jim Womack's E-letters,
Publication Date: 10 Jan, 2003

Womack, P.J., Jones, D.T. (2003),
Lean Thinking,
Simon & Schuster, New York, USA,
ISBN 0-7432-4927-5

Womack, P.J., Jones, D.T., Roos, D. (1990),
The Machine that Changed the World,
Rawson Associates, New York, USA,
ISBN 0-89256-350-8

www.toyota.co.jp

About the Authors

Per Petersson

Per holds a Ph.D. in Production Systems. He has been working with Lean since 1995 in positions such as manufacturing engineer, researcher and manager. During his 11 years at Scania Per participated in the development of the Scania Production System (SPS), some of the time as the SPS Manager at Scania's central SPS department.

Ola Johansson

Ola holds a B.Sc. and has been working with manufacturing and improvement work since 1995. He has held positions such as operator, service technician, director of manufacturing and Lean Manager.

Martin Broman

Martin holds a M.Sc. and has been working as a researcher and consultant since 1998. Martin has primarily worked with manufacturing set-ups, layouts and manufacturing strategies. He has a long experience of coaching internal improvement teams.

Dan Blücher

Dan holds a M.Sc. and has been working with manufacturing and improvement work since 1988. Dan has worked as a consultant and as a Global Lean Manufacturing Expert at Gambro. In addition, he has been the chairman of the Swedish Lean Forum.

Henric Alsterman

Henric holds a Ph.D. in Flexible Manufacturing and has been working with manufacturing and manufacturing development since 1983, as an employee as well as in his own business. Over the years he has held positions such as operator, manufacturing engineer, researcher and manager.

In recent years we, at **Part Development AB**, have been consulting in administration, automotive industry, construction industry, distribution, electric power industry, electronics industry, food industry, healthcare, manufacturing industry, medical industry, municipalities, pharmaceuticals industry, services and textile industry.

(Photo: Martina Huber)

About Part Development AB

Part Development AB was founded in 2005 and is a consultancy firm supporting clients within a number of different branches to improve their operations in order to attain increased competitiveness. Productivity and flexibility are central terms to us.

Our way of working is based on the way of thinking and acting that constitutes the core of Lean. Problems and possibilities are dealt with starting from the firm conviction that the foundation of an efficient operation is based on work with details to affect the whole. An important part of our concept is that Part Development AB should not carry out the actual improvement work but support the clients in their own improvement implementations. In this way the clients' needs for external support are minimized, and the knowledge on the improvements performed stays in the client organization.

In the effort to improve the operations of an organization, their strategies, visions, and customer requirements are translated into a set of demands that are put into practice throughout the entire organization. New ways of thinking and new knowledge are transferred to management and workforce through close cooperation in a project. Based on client needs, Part Development AB can provide coaching, training and education during the project. This is a way to ensure that the improvements will be sustainable.

Part Development AB is also an established partner in education with a broad portfolio of Lean training courses. Our view of raising knowledge is that the best way to learn is by doing. This is why our training courses, as far as possible, contain practical exercises where the clients can apply the new knowledge to their own operations. Part Development AB also performs various kinds of production games, some of which have been developed in-house.

Within Part Development AB we have many years of experience from operations management ranging from the business world to academic research. More information about Part Development AB can be found at www.partdevelopment.com.

Glossary

	5S	Method to create a well-organized and functional workplace. The five elements of 5S are: Sort, Structure, Systematic cleaning, Standardize, and Self-discipline.
	5 Why	Method for root cause analysis. Applying the method 5 Why implies putting the question *Why* to the process five times. The purpose of the method is to find the root cause of a specific deviation.
A	**Accomplished improvements list**	List where the workforce's implemented improvements are documented
	Actual capacity	Capacity that is available in practice. Calculation of actual capacity takes process efficiency into consideration.
	Actual demand signal	Signal to indicate the real customer demand concerning what, how much and when
	Andon	Japanese term for rice lamp. Within Lean, the term is used partly to describe a lamp that signals a need for support and partly to describe a support resource (see Support resource).
	Assets turnover	Financial performance indicator defined as revenue divided by total assets
	Autonomation	English term for Jidoka, see Jidoka
	Availability	Proportion of the planned production time when the process has worked as planned, i.e. when there has been no unplanned stops

B	**Balanced flow**	Flow where the work content is leveled between all resources
	Bottleneck	Resource having lower capacity than current customer demand rate
	Buffer	Defined intermediate storage that exists in order to deliver when the process cannot deliver. A buffer may consist of time or of parts/products.
	Buffer for planned stops	Buffer function aiming to cover for stops where it is known in advance that the process will not be able to deliver
	Built-in quality	Lean principle under the main principle Jidoka. Built-in quality aims to ensure that quality is built into the process so that everything is made right from the beginning.
C	**Change-over time**	The time between the completion of the last part in one batch and the completion of the first approved part in the next batch
	Connection	Agreed set of rules describing how two sequential processes should work together. A connection often, but not necessarily, contains a buffer.
	Consumption buffer	Buffer function aiming to cover for lack of synchronization between processes and for variation in customer demand rate
	Continuous flow	Lean principle under the main principle Just-In-Time (JIT). Continuous flow means that products and materials should be continuously moving along the value stream. In this way the lead time can be minimized.
	Converging flow	Flow where two or more parallel flows merge into one
	Cycle time	Time indicating the frequency at which a product leaves a process

D

Daily control	Daily decision meetings where leaders and members of the workforce decide on actions based on frequent and systematic information about how the operation is doing according to plan and what was the cause of detected deviations
Delivery reliability	The proportion of products that are delivered in time
Deviation	Result or event that deviates from standard, i.e. from what is considered normal
Disturbance buffer	A buffer function aiming to cover for unplanned stops in the delivering process
Diverging flow	Flow that divides into two or more parallel flows
DuPont chart	Financial analysis model indicating what influences the company's return on assets. The DuPont chart considers revenues, costs as well as capital.

F

False customer demand	Unnecessary workload imposed because the work was not correctly carried out in the first place, or because the customer has been kept waiting for too long
FIFO	Short for First In, First Out. FIFO means that all parts leave the flow in exactly the same sequence as they entered into the flow.
Finished goods inventory	Finished products ready for delivery to the customer
Flow	See Value stream
Flow kaizen	Continuous improvements aiming at improving the flow that links the processes together

G	**Genba**	Japanese term for the place where value is added (sometimes spelled Gemba)
	Gross list	List where the employees should note detected deviations. The Gross list is an unsorted register of deviations that have not yet been dealt with.
H	**Heijunka**	Japanese term for leveling meaning that (i) the same quantity of products is planned into each time period, and that (ii) the production sequence is planned so that products/variants with high work contents are separated as much as possible.
I	**Improvement team**	Group of employees who have the responsibility and authority to improve the operation within their assigned areas of responsibility
	Information flow	The flow of information to the product flow as well as to the material flow
	Intermediate storage	Undefined intermediate storage of parts between processes in a flow
J	**Jidoka**	Main principle within Lean aiming to achieve high and predictable quality without the need for inspections. Under Jidoka there are two principles: Built-in quality and Stop the process.
	Just-In-Time (JIT)	Main principle within Lean aiming to achieve short and predictable lead times. Under JIT there are three principles: Takt, Continuous flow and Pull system.
K	**Kaikaku**	Japanese term for radical improvements. Kaikaku is a form of improvement work that is carried out in the project form with clear and quantified goals.

	Kaizen	Japanese term for continuous improvements. Kaizen means continuous improvement work in small and controlled steps and it should constitute the foundation of the improvement work.
	Kaizen Event	Temporary improvement work, where different types of stakeholders are gathered in an intensive workshop. During one or more days the participants from the functions concerned work intensively to solve a particular problem or a particular type of problem.
	Kanban	Japanese term for card or visible evidence. Kanban is also a method to order production or material.
L	**Lead time**	The time it takes for a product to pass through a process or a value stream
	Lean Accounting	Financial control supporting Lean thinking
	Lean principle	Basic way of thinking within Lean that guides the effort to eliminate waste
	Leveling	See Heijunka
	Limiting resource	The process of a flow having the lowest actual capacity
M	**Management by Means**	Operational control focusing on the correct and consequent application of the right ways of working. Management by Means is in contrast to Management by Results.
	Management by Results	Operational control where the results are considered more important than the ways of working. Management by Results is in contrast to Management by Means.
	Material flow	The flow of material to a product flow
	Method	A way of working

MPC system	Manufacturing Planning and Control system
Muda	Japanese term for waste. Muda is often categorized into seven forms of waste: overproduction, waiting, transport, inappropriate processing, inventory, motion, producing defective products. Sometimes these seven forms of waste are extended by an eighth one often called untapped competence.
Mura	Japanese term for unevenness
Muri	Japanese term for overburden

O

OEE	Overall Equipment Effectiveness. OEE is a measure of process efficiency that is adapted to automatic and semi automatic processes.

P

PDCA	Short for Plan, Do, Check and Act. PDCA is a method of structuring improvement work.
PICK chart	Model to prioritize deviations from the criteria effect and effort. PICK is short for Possible, Implement, Challenge and Kill.
Planned production time	The time available for production, defined as available time minus planned stop time
Planned stop	A halt in a process which is known and planned in advance in terms of time of occurrence and duration
Planning point	Point in the flow where decisions are made on what to produce next, i.e. where the production sequence can be changed
Present value	Production review parameter indicating how many products have been produced at a certain point in time
Principle	See Lean principle

Process	Value-adding part of a flow. It is in the processes that work is carried out on the products, and it is the processes that determine the capacity of the flow.
Process efficiency	Performance indicator indicating how much of the planned production time can be used on the average to produce products at the right quality
Process kaizen	Continuous improvements aiming to achieve improvements at process level
Process time	The time it takes for a product to pass through a process, i.e. the lead time of the process
Product flow	The flow of products that are being produced
Production backlog	Situation where the actual production is lower than the planned production
Production flow	The sum of product, material, and information flows
Production sequence	The order (sequence) in which the products pass through the product flow
Pull system	Lean principle under the main principle Just-In-Time (JIT). Pull system means that the customer process signals demand in terms of what, when and how much to the supplying process.
Pulse	Alternative term to represent the follow-up of work progress versus plan in operations where customer demand cannot be easily expressed in numbers of units
Push system	Way to order production where what to produce, how much and when is determined by a central planning activity. Push system is in contrast to Pull system.

R	**Real time**	Conception of time meaning here and now
	Restoration time	Available production time, within normal work hours, intended to be used to restore the production situation so that the production backlog can be eliminated
	Return on assets	Profitability measure defined as the net profit margin multiplied by the assets turnover
	Revealing flow	Flow that is designed so that deviations are easy to detect. In a sense this means that the flow is sensitive to disturbances.
	Root cause	The real cause of a deviation. When the root cause is resolved, the deviation will not recur.
S	**Scrap rate**	The proportion of produced products that have to be scrapped
	Sequence buffer	Buffer function aiming to provide the possibility to create or recreate the desired production sequence
	SMED	Method for change-over time reduction. SMED is short for Single-digit Minute Exchange of Die.
	Standard	Agreement on the best currently known way. Standard is a common term for all kinds of defined agreements.
	Standardized work	Standard describing how a manual work task should be carried out and stating its defined duration
	Stop	Deviation that forces one or more processes to stop
	Stop the process	Lean principle under the main principle Jidoka. Stop the process aims to ensure that the quality problems that come up cannot be passed on in the flow.

Storage time	The time that a buffer or storage will last with current customer demand rate
Storage	Undefined storage of products, parts, etc.
Support function	Organizational function with the assignment to support operations. Examples of common support functions are manufacturing engineering and logistics.
Support resource	Person(s) who on an unplanned basis come(s) to rescue so that an occurred deviation will not stop the process
Synchronized processes	Processes in a flow that are running simultaneously, e.g. processes having the same shift form

T

takt	Decided production volume per time unit (Note! lower-case)
Takt	Lean principle under the main principle Just-In-Time (JIT). Takt sets the pulse that permeates the entire production system and contributes to synchronize all activities.
Takt time	Defined as planned production time divided by the agreed takt. Indicates how often a product should leave the process to fulfill the agreed takt (customer demand)
Target value	Production review parameter indicating how many products should have been produced at a certain point in time according to plan
Total assets	The sum of all assets, i.e. everything from buildings and machinery to accounts receivable and cash

U

Unplanned stop	Stop in a process that cannot be predicted in terms of time of occurrence or duration

V	**Value stream**	The entirety that comprises and connects all processes and activities that a product (physical or not) passes from start to finish. In this book the term value stream is used synonymously with flow.
	Value Stream Mapping	Method to map a value stream and to create a proposal for an improved future value stream
	Variant resource	Person(s) who on a planned basis step(s) in to support work on products/variants with large work contents on stations with high loads
W	**Waste**	Those things, activities, etc. that do not add value and that the customer is not willing to pay for
	WIP	Short for Work In Progress, i.e. products that are partly processed but have not yet left the value stream. WIP is synonymous with WIQ (Work In Queue).
	WIQ	Short for Work In Queue. More relevant synonym of Work In Progress (WIP).

Index

Notes